CIAL SECURITY

Health:
Drinking Sensibly

A discussion document
prepared by the
Health Departments of
Great Britain and
Northern Ireland

HER MAJESTY'S STATIONERY OFFICE

Government Bookshops

49 High Holborn, London WC1V 6HB
13a Castle Street, Edinburgh EH2 3AR
41 The Hayes, Cardiff CF1 1JW
Brazennose Street, Manchester M60 8AS
Southey House, Wine Street, Bristol BS1 2BQ
258 Broad Street, Birmingham B1 2HE
80 Chichester Street, Belfast BT1 4JY

Government publications are also available
through booksellers

ISBN 0 11 320775 1

Contents

Foreword

This booklet is being issued in the United Kingdom Health Departments'
Prevention and Health series because of the considerable problems for the
health of individuals, and our society as a whole, which alcohol misuse pre-
sents. The misuse of alcohol has implications beyond the field of public
health, however. Other issues are raised for our society which cannot be
ignored or treated in isolation. Central to these is the question of the
respective roles individuals and the Government must play in curbing a problem which stems primarily from the exercise by individuals of their freedom of
choice. To help clarify public views, this booklet examines the scope for
action at all levels of society and includes, where appropriate, statements of
the Government's position. We hope that the booklet will be widely read and
discussed.

NORMAN FOWLER
Secretary of State for Social Services

GEORGE YOUNGER
Secretary of State for Scotland

NICHOLAS EDWARDS
Secretary of State for Wales

JAMES PRIOR
Secretary of State for Northern Ireland

CHAPTER I Background

Introduction

Alcohol gives harmless pleasure to many, and most people drink sensibly. But a significant minority drink in such a way as to cause harm to themselves and others—that is to say, they *misuse* alcohol. The aim of this booklet is not to stop people drinking but to encourage sensible attitudes towards the use of alcohol.

Some people choose not to drink, but for the majority drinking is a pleasure which enlivens many a social occasion. Unfortunately, there is another side. For some people alcohol causes major problems. It damages their own lives and the lives of those around them. Misuse of alcohol can be a major cause of mental illness, of disrupted families and of inefficiency at work. It also contributes more than is generally recognised, to a wide range of physical illnesses. The effects spread far beyond the drinkers and their immediate circle. Burdens are put on health and social services for which we all pay, as well as on commerce and industry. Misuse of alcohol contributes to criminal behaviour and to the workloads of the courts and the prisons. And drink causes accidents, fatal or disabling, in the home, on the roads, and at work.

The problem of alcohol misuse has recently attracted much attention. In 1975 an Advisory Committee on Alcoholism was set up by the DHSS and the Welsh Office and produced 3 reports—the first of which, in 1977, was on prevention. A similar report was issued by the Scottish Council on Alcoholism in 1978. In 1977, the Expenditure Committee of the House of Commons made a number of proposals on alcohol in its report on preventive medicine. In 1979, a Special Committee of the Royal College of Psychiatrists made proposals in its report 'Alcohol and Alcoholism' and in 1980 problems related to alcohol consumption were considered by an Expert Committee of the World Health Organisation. One fact they all stressed is that alcohol misuse is growing.

The Health Departments have prepared this booklet to present a balanced overall picture of the Government's policies on the health and social issues related to alcohol misuse. The booklet does not suggest that the use of alcohol is in itself undesirable. It simply describes the extent of misuse, the types of harm misuse of alcohol can cause, the costs to society and the ways individuals and the Government can act. The object is to widen understanding of the problems and to encourage sensible attitudes.

Responsible citizens must consider in the light of these facts what they themselves can do to limit the harm to their own health and the health of others and whether they think the Government should do more to minimise alcohol misuse and to counter its effects. The scope for Government to influence social habits is limited and the effects of such action on personal behaviour must always be uncertain; but informed public discussion will help the Government to decide what policies to follow in this important and sensitive field.

The scope for action summarised

The problems are complex. Many aspects of private and public life are involved. Alcohol gives considerable pleasure as well as causing, for a minority, considerable harm. Every society which uses alcohol controls its use in one or more ways—social, legal and fiscal. These controls have consequences for social life as well as for the economy.

Some observers believe that the most important controls are those which are social and which indicate by custom the circumstances in which alcohol may be drunk, and in what quantity. Where these social controls are strong, where alcohol is drunk moderately in appropriate circumstances and where drunkenness is frowned upon, levels of problem drinking tend to be low. In societies where opposite attitudes and practices are found problem drinking tends to be common.

Governments attempt to influence the use of alcohol more directly by laws governing the distribution and availability of alcohol. Public order and public safety considerations are influential. But in this country, there have been in the last 2 centuries many amendments of the law relating to drink, which were aimed at reducing the medical, social and economic effects of misuse. The laws relating to opening hours and to the admission of young people to public houses are examples. Intervention on these grounds is not new; in the 1720s the Royal College of Physicians appealed to the Government to stop the sale of gin at cheap rates, which was giving rise to sickness and public disorder on a large scale.

Although taxation has also been used to limit consumption, the primary purpose of duties on alcoholic drinks remains, as in most countries, to raise revenue. The Government must also have regard to the economic importance of the drinks industry and the licensed trade and to the interests of those working in them. It is necessary to balance the arguments; to consider with care all the effects of measures designed to limit the harm caused by alcohol misuse; and to ensure that such measures do not have a disproportionate outcome for employment and trade or the social behaviour of the majority.

This booklet considers measures—social, legal and fiscal—which might curb alcohol misuse. In each case, it tries to set out the effects which a particular measure might be expected to have apart from the likely health and social benefits.

None of the courses mentioned is straightforward, or without effects on other areas; none can be looked at wholly in isolation. Moreover, whatever the Government may do, controls must be applied by individuals themselves. Where the Government does act, it can in general do so effectively only with the broad assent of the public. What happens when Governments get out of step with a substantial body of opinion was amply demonstrated by the experience of prohibition in the USA early this century. It is, therefore, essential that there should be as wide an understanding as possible of what are the facts and what are the possibilities for improvement—and, equally, what are the likely effects on us now and for future generations if no action, or inadequate action, is taken and current trends in the misuse of alcohol continue.

The range of possible courses is therefore wide. The Government hopes that this booklet will inform, will stimulate discussion and will help a climate of opinion to evolve within which such further measures as may gain public support or acceptance may be effectively taken.

CHAPTER II The effects of alcohol misuse

Definition

Alcohol misuse means drinking to excess or drinking in situations which are not appropriate, when the effect in either case is to put the drinker or others at risk of harm. Harm may arise from alcohol-related impairment (intoxication), alcohol-related disabilities, or alcohol dependence.

Alcohol-related impairment (which is temporary) means the dulling of senses and loosening of normal inhibitions which immediately follow drinking. Even small degrees of impairment can be crucial and can result in accidental injuries or death. Greater impairment can lead to drunkenness in public, can be a cause of serious road traffic accidents and can contribute to hooliganism and vandalism, violent crimes, and absenteeism from work.

Alcohol-related disabilities encompass the more lasting consequences of misuse, such as physical and mental disorders, damaged work and career opportunities, and marital and family problems arising from the financial and other personal implications of heavy drinking.

Persistent heavy alcohol misuse may lead to addiction or dependence. Dependence is an important feature of what is often called 'alcoholism', a term which is frequently used without precise meaning. The 'alcohol dependence syndrome' is a concept which defines elements of dependence more precisely.*

---

* Footnote: The Term 'alcoholism' is used in places in this booklet, but only where dependence is meant. The 'alcohol dependence syndrome' has replaced 'alcoholism' in the ninth revision of the International Classification of Diseases and is now preferred by the World Health Organisation. The WHO Technical Report 'Problems related to alcohol consumption' summarises the main features of the syndrome as 'a changed behavioural state in an individual that includes, in addition to an alteration in overt drinking behaviour, a continuation of drinking in a way not approved of in his culture, despite painful direct consequences, such as physical illness, rejection by his family, economic embarrassment and penal sanctions.' There is also 'an altered subjective state, in which the dependent person's control over his drinking is impaired, there is a craving for drink, and an element of 'drink centredness' is manifested, whereby the planning of his drinking may take precedence over that of other activities. In addition to the above changes, an altered psychobiological state is noted, with experience of signs and symptons of withdrawal, drinking for relief of withdrawal, and increased tolerance.'

Patterns of misuse

Misuse through drinking to excess means either bouts of drunkenness involving rapid intoxication over a short period ('binge' drinking) or prolonged drinking—that is regular heavy consumption over a long period. The former can in extreme cases result in death through alcohol poisoning, through choking on vomit, or through accidents; the latter can lead to accidents, long-term disabilities and eventual dependence. Examples of situations where drinking is inappropriate are before driving or some other potentially dangerous or demanding activity. Only a small amount of alcohol, particularly if taken on an empty stomach, may be sufficient to cause impairment and make people a danger to themselves and to others.

Immediate effects of alcohol

The immediate effects of alcoholic beverages are mainly due to ethyl alcohol, or ethanol, which is to be found in roughly equal quantities in a half pint of beer, a glass of table wine, or in a single measure of spirits such as gin, vodka, or whisky. When absorbed into the blood, ethanol will normally increase the heart rate, dilate the blood vessels causing flushing and a feeling of warmth, and stimulate the flow of gastric juices. Above all it affects the nervous system and the brain. Ethanol acts as a nervous system depressant—not a stimulant as is commonly believed. It depresses the parts of the brain which control and to some extent inhibit behaviour. It impairs the senses, bodily co-ordination, the ability to judge distance, memory, judgement, the ability to react to changing situations, and concentration. The loss of control and sense of euphoria tends to encourage further drinking. The effect of alcohol in the early stages is often to convince the drinker that he is performing better although his faculties are actually being impaired. Later he may be beyond caring. With further drinking, the brain function will be depressed to the extent that the drinker is less rational, more clumsy and appears drunk to others. Ultimately, if sufficient alcohol is consumed, brain activity is so depressed that the drinker may become unconscious or even die from paralysis of centres controlling such vital functions as breathing, swallowing and circulation.

The adverse effects will vary in degree according to how much is consumed and in what circumstances. The effect will be less if alcohol is consumed gradually, over a fairly long period, or is drunk at meal times with food. The effects may also be less in a heavy person or experienced drinker. Impairment will be aggravated if alcohol is taken on an empty stomach or rapidly over a short period of time, or in the case of a lightweight person or an inexperienced drinker. Furthermore, if alcohol and certain drugs (eg sleeping tablets, antihistamines, tranquillisers of anti-depressants) are taken together the effects of both in combination are likely to be highly dangerous.

Long-term effects

The effects described above are generally short-lived. Normal faculties are regained once the alcohol has left the body, a process which takes time and depends on the amount consumed. However, prolonged heavy drinking over months or years may result in lasting and possibly irreversible damage. Such drinking may not lead to obvious drunkenness. But a high alcohol intake over a long period generally leads to an insidious build-up of permanent harmful effects. Heavy drinkers may find that they become increasingly tolerant to alcohol, and cannot do without it, and need to drink more and more to produce the same effect. Eventually, they may reach the stage where, because their constitution has become so used to coping with a constant high level of alcohol, any appreciable *lessening* of intake will bring on unpleasant withdrawal symptons. These may include sweating, anxiety and trembling, and even convulsions, delirium, delirium tremens (DTs) and coma. These may all be relieved by more alcohol. So the process is self-generating.

Health problems from heavy drinking

Alcohol can be a causative or complicating factor in many illnesses for which specialist treatment is required as well as in many minor ailments treated by general practitioners. In several studies carried out in the United Kingdom in recent years between 15 and 30% of men admitted to general medical, orthopaedic, and casualty departments in hospitals were found to be either problem drinkers or physically dependent on alcohol.

Nutritional and digestive troubles may be the first signs of illness resulting from prolonged heavy drinking. Although alcoholic drinks contain small amounts of iron, calcium and magnesium and some of the B vitamins, their principal food value is as a source of energy. Consequently, if alcohol is drunk in large quantities on top of a normal diet, obesity—with its own risks—may result. However, alcohol is sometimes consumed by heavy drinkers instead of normal foods. Serious nutritional deficiencies may follow and may be aggravated by the loss of appetite caused by inflammation of the stomach (gastritis) and the impairment of absorption from the gut caused by irritation of the bowel lining. Vomiting, nausea, loss of appetite and diarrhoea are commonly occurring warning signs of damage.

Cirrhosis of liver is probably the best known long-term physical consequence of excessive drinking. This is a progressive and potentially lethal disease in which damaged cells are replaced by fibrous tissues. Although alcohol is not the sole cause of liver cirrhosis, it is thought to account for over one half of cases and it is known that women are particularly susceptible.

Apart from the liver and digestive systems many other parts of the body may be affected by prolonged heavy drinking. Chest diseases such as chronic bronchitis, pneumonia, pulmonary tuberculosis, may occur more frequently, whilst disease of the heart muscle, disease of body muscle, and impairment of the bone marrow's ability to produce normal red cells may all be caused by alcohol. Certain cancers such as those of the throat, gullet and stomach may occur more frequently in association with heavy alcohol use.

Diseases of the nervous system are common in problem drinkers. Inflammation of the nerves to the arms and legs leading to loss of power, sensation and co-ordination may occur as a result of vitamin deficiencies caused by the heavy use of alcohol.

Brain damage may also occur in this way and there is growing concern that shrinkage of the brain and intellectual impairment may occur more frequently and at an earlier stage than previously thought, as a result of the direct toxic effects of alcohol.

Heavy drinking may also lead to anxiety and agitation, depression, sexual problems, paranoia, memory black-outs and hallucinations.

Effects of alcohol on the fetus

There is evidence that excessive drinking during pregnancy can damage the unborn child but the extent of the drinking necessary to cause such damage is such that it would be advisable on health grounds to reduce the intake greatly irrespective of pregnancy. Very few cases have been reported in this country, but it is clearly important that mothers-to-be should be moderate in their use of alcohol on general health grounds.

Premature deaths and suicides

Alcohol misuse can lead to untimely death. The death rate on a comparative age basis among people who have become dependent on alcohol is twice as high as that of the adult population at large, and the difference is particularly great in young age groups. Studies have shown a very high level of suicide and attempted suicide by problem drinkers. There is also a higher incidence of death from accidents, poisoning and violence in this group. In 1979, of some 400 drownings in England and Wales reported to the Home Office which specified contributory causes, 'alcohol' was mentioned in 30% of cases reported. Alcohol has also been shown to be a factor in fatal falls and deaths in fires in the home, but although it is assumed to play an important part in domestic accidents generally, there is as yet little systematic information on this.

Road traffic accidents

Perhaps the most widely recognised social aspect of alcohol misuse is 'drinking and driving' and the part alcohol plays in road traffic accidents. Alcohol dulls people's sense of judgement, essential when driving, yet at the same time distorts their perception of their own abilities. Several important studies have shown that, however drinking drivers may assess their own capabilities, in reality, the more they drink before driving, the greater the risk of a road accident—an accident which may involve not only the driver but passengers and other road users. A pedestrian who is under the influence of alcohol could also be at greater risk of involvement in a road accident. Some 20-25% of adult pedestrians killed in Great Britain are found to have a blood/alcohol level in excess of 80 mg of alcohol per 100 ml of blood.

It is estimated that one in five of all road deaths is related to excessive drinking. Road accidents cause roughly half of all male deaths between the ages of 15 and 24, and the largest factor in these casualties is alcohol.

Accidents at work and effects on employment

People whose judgement is impaired even temporarily by drink are a danger to the health and safety of themselves, their work mates and their employers, and to others who may be affected by their work activities. As with accidents in the home there is scope for further investigation, but it has been shown that alcohol does play a part in industrial accidents. Its role has not always been recognised because many other factors may contribute to accidents at the work place and because those involved may be reluctant to admit that drink was a factor.

Many problem drinkers are in regular employment. They inevitably bring their problems to the work place. In one survey of problem drinkers roughly one-tenth were certain that their drinking had been responsible for an accident, and a further one-third thought it might have been a factor. Habitual heavy drinking may also have serious consequences for employment prospects, due to poor work performance, frequent absence and sickness, and inability to retain steady or skilled employment. For the drinker's employer the picture is one of unreliability, inefficiency, and lost output; for work mates it is one of unpredictable behaviour, and the need to cover up for poor performance.

Violence and crime

As alcohol lessens inhibitions and to an extent weakens people's self control it may in some individuals and in some situations lead directly to violence and crime. Links between drinking and acts of vandalism and hooliganism have been shown, particularly by young people in groups, as at football matches. A number of studies have been carried out on alcohol and serious crime, although few have been designed to assess the extent to which drinking contributes directly to the commission of criminal offences. In 1979, in England and Wales, there were over 114,000 court appearances where a person was found guilty of drunkenness offences, including over 11,000 cases where the defendant was found guilty of another, possibly more serious, offence. Other studies have shown that varying and sometimes substantial proportions of violent offenders had been drinking at the time they committed the offence.

Family life

Heavy drinking may affect family life in a variety of ways. The heavy drinker may spend a large proportion of the family income on alcohol and much of his or her leisure time drinking away from home, leaving the family to manage as best they can. As the drinker's behaviour is likely to be unpredictable it puts further strain on domestic relationships. Violent out-bursts may occur. 'Wife battering' is often associated with alcohol abuse; the part that alcohol may play in child abuse is less clear.

The problem drinker will probably become increasingly isolated emotionally from the family. The family too may become socially isolated, and ashamed to invite people home or to talk about their problems. Children may be forced to take up sides between parents. They may despise the drinking parent or may themselves grow up to become problem drinkers. Eventually, marriages and families may break up. Although the effect on home life cannot be measured, many professionals in the health and personal social services consider this to be one of the most serious long-term problems of alcohol misuse.

The wide ranging effects of alcohol misuse on the health and quality of life of individuals and their families, and on performance at work and industrial output, make it one of today's major social problems. It affects directly or indirectly the great majority of the population, not least because of the health and social resources that are diverted from less preventable forms of illness and social problems. The costs to the wider community are further explored in the following chapter.

CHAPTER III The costs of misuse

Size of the problem

We cannot tell precisely how many people have serious drinking problems.*
There are difficulties in definition, and, to date, there have been no national
surveys into the extent of alcohol misuse (though surveys into *drinking habits*
were carried out in Scotland in 1972, in England and Wales in 1978, and in
Northern Ireland in 1978). Estimates of the number of people dependent on
alcohol are needed to help with the effective planning of services and allo-
cation of resources. The best approach to gauging the size of the problem and
trends over time lies in monitoring certain indicators of 'harm'. These include
such data as hospital admissions for alcoholism and related diseases; deaths
from these conditions; convictions for drunkenness and 'drink and driving'
offences; and the proportion of drivers killed in road traffic accidents with
blood/alcohol levels above the legal limit. It is significant that over recent
years, all these indicators have been moving together and have been showing a
serious and deteriorating situation.

The assessment of the size of the social problem has also to take account of
the additional dimension of those directly affected by the problem drinker,
including family, friends and work mates.

Hospital admissions

Figure 1 shows that from 1965 to 1979 the number of patients admitted to
hospital with a primary diagnosis of alcoholism or alcoholic psychosis more

*Footnote: Estimates were made by the Office of Population Censuses and Surveys in 1979,
intended to give only a broad indication of prevalence and of trends over time. They suggested
a 50% increase in the number of people in the United Kingdom with serious drinking problems
over the 10 years to 1977 (from about half million to about three-quarters million). The special
committee of the Royal College of Psychiatrists, in its report in 1979, agreed the scale of the
increase and their conservative estimate was at least 300,000 people with severe drinking
problems. The 1980 OPCS Survey on Drinking in England and Wales found that 5% of men
and 2% of women in the survey had drinking problems. The number of people dependent on
alcohol has been put at 70,000 by Griffith Edwards in evidence to the House of Commons
Expenditure Committee in 1976 and at around 240,000 by the OPCS.

Figure 1. Admissions to Mental Illness Hospitals and Units of Patients with a primary
diagnosis of Alcoholism or Alcoholic Psychosis, 1965 - 1979.*
United Kingdom.

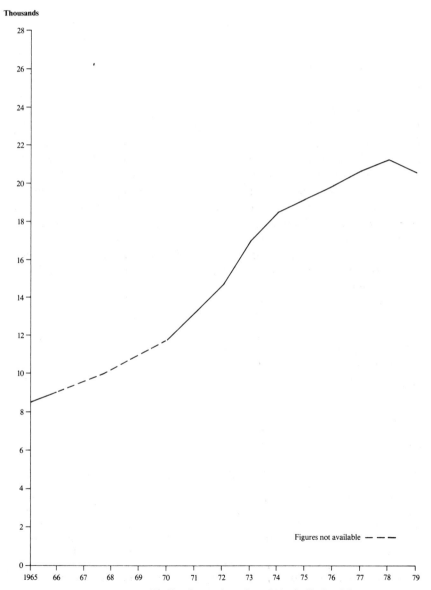

*Figures for 1979 are not fully comparable with earlier years due to changes in the classification of diseases.

than doubled in the United Kingdom. There was a greater rise in Northern Ireland and in England and Wales than in Scotland. The *rate* of admissions is appreciably higher in Northern Ireland (137:100,000 in 1979) and in Scotland (97:100,000) than in England and Wales (27:100,000). It is difficult to judge how far these trends represent an increasing incidence of alcoholism and alcohol psychosis. They may reflect better provision of treatment facilities, more accurate diagnosis, a greater willingness on the part of problem drinkers to seek treatment, or changes in the size or composition of the general population. Most probably a combination of all these factors is the explanation. But, whatever the reason, it cannot be denied that there has been a sharp rise in recent years in the number of recorded cases of problem drinkers receiving specialist treatment from the NHS.

Deaths from alcoholism and liver cirrhosis

The numbers of deaths attributed to alcoholism and to liver cirrhosis—one of the key indicators of the incidence of chronic alcohol misuse—may not seem high when compared with deaths from cancers, heart disease, and accidents (which account for about 75% of all deaths). They do not reflect, however, the full extent to which alcohol is a factor in fatal diseases or in morbidity generally, and their particular importance is as indicators of trends over time in the incidence of chronic alcohol misuse. Figure 2 shows the trends in the United Kingdom since 1964. Since the early 1970s the number of deaths from alcoholism has risen sharply in England and Wales and Scotland, but the same trend has not been seen in Northern Ireland. Scotland has a much higher death rate from alcoholism (approximately 4.3 deaths per 100,000 population in 1978) than Northern Ireland (approximately 0.9 per 100,000) or England and Wales (approximately 0.4 per 100,000). Cirrhosis deaths have increased more or less steadily since 1964, but since 1970 the number recorded has risen sharply. The increase has been equally marked among men and women. The figures are relatively worse in Scotland (7.4 cirrhosis deaths per 100,000 population in 1978) than in Northern Ireland (3.6 per 100,000) and England and Wales (3.9 per 100,000). The trend in both alcoholism and cirrhosis deaths doubtless reflects factors such as population changes and improved diagnosis. But when the overall trends are taken in conjunction with the other indicators available it is difficult to avoid the conclusion that increased alcohol misuse is likely to account for by far the greater part of the rise.

Findings of guilt for drunkenness offences

Figure 3 shows the trend in findings of guilt for offences of drunkenness in England and Wales since 1970 separately for males and females in each age group. The sharp rise in the figures for young people, young women as well as

Figure 2. Deaths from Cirrhosis of the Liver and Alcoholism.
United Kingdom.

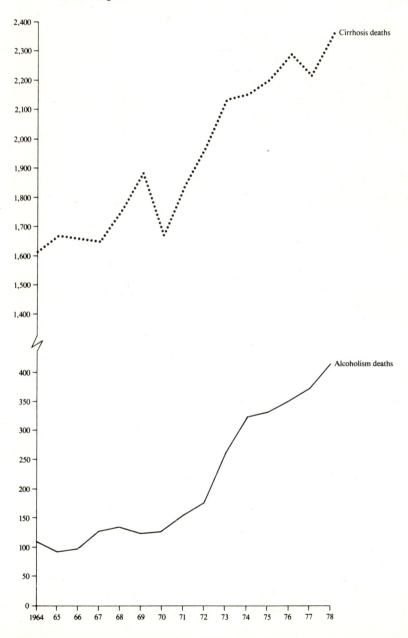

men, over the last 10 years is particularly noticeable. The number of findings of guilt may be affected by changes in, for example, police priorities or manpower levels, but the evidence does suggest that in recent years public displays of drunkenness among the young have increased. The same consistently upward trend seen in England and Wales since 1970 has not been seen in Scotland or Northern Ireland, but the position is not strictly comparable because of differences in the law.

Figure 3. Findings of guilt for offences of drunkenness per 100,000 population in age
groups, 1970 - 1980.
England and Wales.

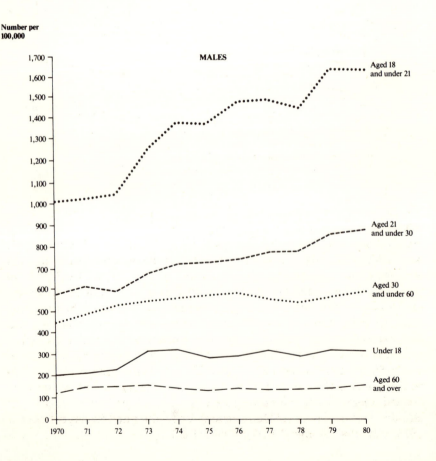

Figure 3 (continued). Findings of guilt for offences of drunkenness per 100,000 population in age groups, 1970 - 1980. England and Wales.

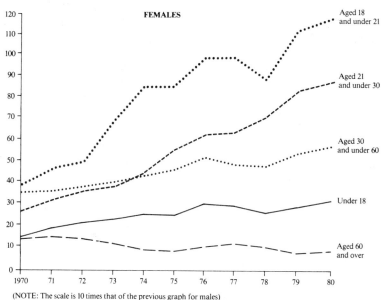

(NOTE: The scale is 10 times that of the previous graph for males)

Findings of guilt for drink and driving offences

Figure 4 shows the number of findings of guilt in England and Wales annually since 1968 for driving or being in charge of a vehicle while unfit through drink or a drug, or while having a blood/alcohol level above the legal limit. In practice, very few findings of guilt relate to driving while unfit due to a drug, the vast majority of offences being alcohol-related. The graph shows a rising trend to 1975, followed by a fall for 2 years—which may indicate a real improvement or may reflect in part other pressures competing for police attention—Findings of guilt in England and Wales increased again in 1978 to nearly 58,000 and to almost 67,000 in 1979. In 1978 they totalled over 10,000 in Scotland, a higher rate in relation to the size of the population. In Northern Ireland where evidential procedures and penalties differ from those in Great Britain, there were over 4,700 convictions for drinking and driving offences in 1978, more than double the 1968 figure (1,800).

Figure 4. Findings of guilt for driving etc. after consuming alcohol or taking drugs, 1968 - 1978.
England and Wales.

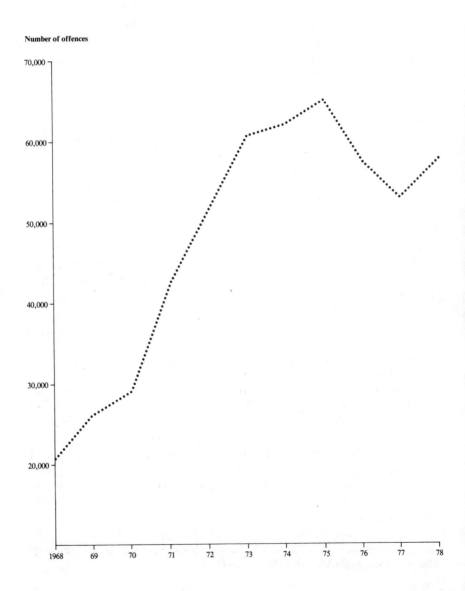

Deaths in road traffic accidents

A more reliable indicator of the extent of drinking and driving is the proportion of the drivers killed in accidents who are found to have a blood/alcohol level above the legal limit. This proportion is a more significant indicator because, unlike the number of convictions, it is not influenced directly by variations in police enforcement policy or manpower levels (although, of course, the public perception of police activity may have an effect on the local incidence of drinking and driving, and ultimately on the number of fatal accidents). The proportion of vehicle drivers and riders killed in road traffic accidents in England and Wales who had a blood/alcohol level above the legal limit fell sharply from 27% in 1967 when the 'breath test' was introduced to 17% in 1968. It then rose steadily to 35% in 1975 after which it dropped back and in 1980 was provisionally 31%.

A much higher proportion of drivers who have drunk above the limit are killed in road accidents at night after 10.00 pm and particularly on Friday and Saturday nights. Younger drivers, who tend to do more night driving and to be less experienced both as drivers and as drinkers have consistently been the most numerous victims.

Women

Although men account for the majority of admissions to hospital for alcoholism, of deaths from alcoholism or cirrhosis, and of convictions for drunkenness and drink and driving offences, there has been in recent years a particularly marked increase in the number of women involved under all these headings.*

The number of cases of women admitted to hospital in the United Kingdom with a primary diagnosis of alcoholism or alcoholic psychosis increased from over 1,600 in 1965 to nearly 5,700 in 1979. The comparable figures for men were 7,000 and 14,900.

In 1965 23 women died from alcoholism and just over 800 from liver cirrhosis in the United Kingdom. In 1978 126 women died from alcoholism and almost 1,100 from cirrhosis.

The number of findings of guilt for drunkenness offences committed by women in England and Wales rose from over 5,000 in 1969 to over 9,400 in 1979. (The comparable figures for men were, however, 75,400 and 108,000).

---

*Footnote: In the OPCS survey of drinking in England and Wales, however, only 3% of women were classified as heavy drinkers and only 1% had drunk more than 35 units of alcohol in the past week, compared in both cases to 14% of men.

Alcoholism counselling agencies report that an increasing number of women—especially young women—are asking for help. One in 2.4 of all applicants at local councils on alcoholism in England and Wales in 1980/81 were women, compared to 1 in 4 in 1974.

Economic costs

The personal suffering from alcohol related disease and the stress experienced by the relatives and friends of problem drinkers and those who have come into conflict with the law as a result of drinking cannot be easily measured or quantified in money terms. Nor can the true costs to the NHS be calculated of the treatment of all the conditions which may be induced or aggravated by misuse of alcohol. Further work is required, particularly on the prevalence of problem drinking and on the amount of sickness absence from work which is alcohol-related, before reliable estimates can be made of costs.*

Trends abroad

The trends shown by the indicators of alcohol-related harm so far described are not peculiar to the United Kingdom. They are a common experience in many other countries including the developing as well as the developed nations. International comparisons are difficult to make but liver cirrhosis death rates probably indicate the trends reasonably accurately. Although consumption of alcohol is not the sole cause of liver cirrhosis it is likely to be the main cause of variation in cirrhosis death rates. The death rates from cirrhosis increased for men in 24, and for women in 17 out of 26 countries between the late 1950s and 1974. The change in the United Kingdom in that period was about average but, exceptionally and excluding Scotland, the death rate for women increased faster than that for men. Cirrhosis death rates in the United Kingdom remain well below those seen in many other countries. But this is no reason for complacency nor for failing to respond to increases in alcohol-related harm before the problem becomes critical, as it has done in some other European countries.

---

*Footnote: Estimates have been made, however, of the material cost of accidents at work or on the road, their resource impact on health and personal social services, the police and the courts; the resource costs of certain other identified uses made of health and personal social services; and the costs of loss of output due to sickness, unemployment or premature deaths. A preliminary study of the cost to society of alcohol misuse in 1977 carried out by economists in the Department of Health and Social Security suggests that these quantifiable items totalled between £425m and £650m (in England and Wales), at November 1977 prices.

The low and high estimates reflect different assumptions of prevalence (see the footnote on page 16).

CHAPTER IV Causes of misuse

Introduction
There is no simple answer to the question why people misuse alcohol. Problem drinkers include men and women, young and old, introverts and extroverts, rich and poor. Their background may be stable and contented, or insecure and unhappy. They may have successful, rewarding careers, or they may work in unskilled monotonous jobs. Any person who drinks can develop a drinking problem.

Similarly no specific factors can be singled out as leading inevitably either to prolonged heavy drinking or simply to intermittent alcohol misuse. Nonetheless, some of the main factors that influence people first to drink and then to misuse alcohol have been identified. They can be grouped into biological and family influences; social and cultural influences; and personality and environmental influences.

Nature and nurture
Heredity plays a considerable part in determining human behaviour and it may be that some people are genetically predisposed to become dependent on alcohol as others are, say, to contract heart disease. A greater susceptibility to become dependent may be related to differences in the way alcohol is metabolised. This could account for the finding that children of people dependent on alcohol have themselves had high rates of problem drinking even though they have been reared away from their natural parents. The evidence is however inconclusive and it remains difficult to distinguish between genetic and environmental influences.

If the effects of alcohol differ from person to person this may account for the different levels of alcohol-related harm observed in different people with similar alcohol intakes. Just as some, but not all, ciagarette smokers develop lung cancer so some, but not all, heavy drinkers are susceptible, for example, to cirrhosis of the liver. This greater susceptibility may reflect differences in the way that alcohol is metabolised or it may be that with some individuals prolonged heavy drinking simply activates a latent predisposition to harm.

There is a suggestion that the immunological processes of the body may be involved and this could explain why women are more prone to alcohol-related diseases—particularly cirrhosis of the liver—than men.

The family has a strong influence on the attitudes of the young to alcohol, and in the shaping of patterns of drinking. Roughly one half of young people of both sexes are likely to take their first drink at home where it will be provided by their parents. Home is where they will usually drink and it is here by example and precept that they will learn the ways in which alcohol can safely be used in our society. A child who grows up in a family where one or both parents drink heavily may regard this as normal and acceptable behaviour to be emulated in due course, but will also be aware of the emotional distress which accompanies such drinking and may react against these parental standards. Either way children from such families will not readily learn the way in which alcohol is used sensibly and moderately. Children from households where alcohol is strictly forbidden have similar difficulties which may explain why proportionately more problem drinkers come from either teetotal or heavy drinking families.

Social and cultural influences
Custom and cultural factors play a significant part in shaping people's drinking patterns. People seem more likely to drink heavily where this is accepted or even admired than where it is frowned upon. There has long been, for example, a tradition of hard drinking, particularly of whisky, among men in Scotland. The cultural pressures to drink for social acceptance and to drink heavily are likely to be that much greater in Scotland than in England, and this is reflected in a higher level of alcohol-related harm. In Northern Ireland, where there is a strong temperance tradition, a recent survey established that 40% of the population abstained from alcohol, 37% being life-long abstainers. Different cultural attitudes exist also within England. In the North, for example, the proportion of household expenditure devoted to alcohol appears to be half as much again as it is in East Anglia. There may also be sub- cultural differences in patterns of drinking in the same geographical area. Thus, there is likely to be a greater proportion of abstainers in areas where muslim communities have been established and where cultural influences remain strong, and low consumption per head within Jewish communities who disapprove of excessive public drinking. Conversely, the Irish in England as a group drink more heavily and suffer a higher rate of alcohol-related harm than the rest of the population. Contact between cultures over time tends, however, to break down culture patterns in minorities, whose drinking habits may then move towards those of the majority.

There is no doubt that in all parts of the United Kingdom, the numerically largest increases in indicators of harm relate to men, but social changes affecting women and young people may have contributed to the disproportionately rapid increases in alcohol-related harm for these groups. Drinking by women and the young has become much more accepted. As women have become financially less dependent, and less inhibited by social constraints, so their drinking styles and hence their misuse of alcohol have in some ways become more like those of men. Other developments in recent years may also have affected women more than men. A survey of Scottish drinking habits found 91% of the current generation of mothers drank as compared with only 24% of mothers aged 51 and over. Wider acceptability has been accompanied by a growth in the number of outlets where drink can be bought and served—for instance, family pubs, disco bars, wine bars and premises, including supermarkets, where alcohol is sold alongside other domestic provisions.

The World Health Organisation has pointed to the tendency for international patterns of drinking to become established as more people travel abroad on business and holiday. The increase in wine consumption in the United Kingdom (see page 28) may be partly due to this effect and there has also been a growing habit of drinking in settings additional to the traditional public house. New drinks have generally been consumed in addition to rather than in substitution for the traditional beverages.

Drinking patterns in the young

Several factors probably contribute towards the drinking patterns of young people. Most young people who are working have few financial commitments before marriage and they can afford to spend much of their income on themselves. Indeed, a 1978 study of school children's attitudes found that only 3% of both sexes thought alcohol was too expensive for them. Pressures to conform also tended to be higher among young people. 'Because all my friends drink' was a common reason for drinking given by school children.

Young people without domestic ties tend more than other age groups to seek outside entertainment which, even when not directly related to alcohol, may involve incidental drinking, for example, at football matches or at discos. Another factor is that public houses by providing dancing and other entertainments and a variety of food and drink, are becoming more attractive to young people particularly where no other rival entertainment is available locally. For whatever reasons, it seems that more young people are drinking more often and at an earlier age, and that as a group they have established a greater than average increase in such indicators of alcohol-related harm as drunkenness offences and deaths through alcohol-related road traffic accidents.

The 1972 survey of Scottish drinking habits found that for both sexes 'regular drinkers' were most common amongst those aged 17-21 (88% of the males, 64% of the females) and only slightly less common in the 22-30 age group (86% and 58% respectively). Thereafter the proportion of regular drinkers declined steadily with age. The 1978 survey of drinking habits in England and Wales found a much higher proportion of heavy drinkers among the age group 18-24 than in other age groups.

Personality and environmental influences

Many people see drink as a way of escape. The desire to escape may be strongly influenced by social conditions such as poor or overcrowded living accommodation, unemployment, dull or unpleasant work, or other forms of stress and strain. The housewife at home all day may seek relief from loneliness. Those who have suffered a shattering experience such as bereavement or a break with family or partner may seek solace in alcohol.

Personality traits may contribute to patterns of heavy drinking. Shy people may drink to help them mix socially whilst those who are outgoing and gregarious may find that they are expected to drink by the company they keep.

Occupational risks

The nature of a person's job may of itself contribute to or encourage heavy drinking habits. It has long been recognised that people in certain occupations are more 'at risk' than others. Ease of access to alcohol is an understandable factor in the development of drinking problems in publicans and people in the drink and catering trades. The reason why some professional and occupational groups—such as medical practitioners, ships officers, soldiers, miners and financiers, are particularly at risk is less clear but stress, irregular working hours, difficult working conditions, absence of supervision, lack of restraining social influences and monotony are among the factors which could be implicated. On the other hand certain occupations which offer ease of access to alcohol may attract people who already have a drinking problem.

National consumption trends

Complex personal and social factors may not in themselves be sufficient to account for marked increases in misuse and alcohol-related harm and it is important to look also at trends in the consumption per head of alcohol in the country as a whole. In 1980, consumption of beer, spirits and wine per head of population aged 15 and over was respectively some 157, 6½ and 11 litres. These figures represent increases since 1960 of respectively 48, 4 and 8 litres; or, in terms of pure alcohol, 1.7, 1.5 and 0.8 litres.* In spite of these increases, wine consumption remains low in relation to many other European countries and we come eighth in the world league of beer consumers.

This growth in consumption could be accounted for statistically by a decline in the proportion of teetotallers or by a modest increase in the consumption of moderate drinkers. It is significant, however, that as consumption per head has risen so too have the indicators of harm described in Chapter III.

A large number of studies indicate that there is a positive correlation between movements in consumption per head and the trends in cirrhosis death rates—with the notable exception of mortality rates from liver cirrhosis in England and Wales between 1931 and 1945**—and also in the other indicators of harm described in Chapter III. There is evidence—other than that exception—of a decline in any index of alcohol-related harm while a nation's consumption per head has been increasing.

There is also evidence that as consumption per head increases what changes is the amount of alcohol consumed by regular drinkers per drinking day, rather than the proportion of abstainers or the number of occasions on which people take a drink. The World Health Organisation has concluded that 'changes in the overall consumption of alcoholic beverages have a bearing on the health of the people in any society'. The experience in other countries tends to confirm the link between total alcohol consumption and harm. What this implies is that, when total consumption increases, the increase is distributed, to some extent at least, in increased consumption at every level of drinking, with some who had a previously high, but tolerable, level of drinking becoming problem drinkers. Although other explanations have been offered, this provides for many people the most convincing explanation for the strikingly parallel changes that there have been in rates of consumption and harm.

Prevention

The Expenditure Committee of the House of Commons, the Advisory Committee on Alcoholism, a Special Committee of the Royal College of Psychiatrists, and an Expert Committee of the World Health Organisation

---

*Footnote: There has been a more recent reported decline in consumption, possibly due to economic recession. Firm information is not available and it will be some time before it is known whether any current decline represents more than an interruption of a longer term general trend.

**Footnote: Studies suggest this is caused by a time lag between changes in consumption and cirrhosis mortality.

have in recent years all considered and made recommendations on ways of preventing growth in alcohol misuse and related harm.* Each has distinguished between the roles which the Government and the individual can play, and identified measures for the Government to consider. The response to the Expenditure Committee's recommendations published by the Government in 1977 (Prevention and Health: Cmnd 7047) pointed to the need for greater public discussion of possible remedies. The following chapters consider in detail the recommendations made by the Expenditure Committee and by the other reports, and set out the Government's response.

---

*Footnote: These are summarised in Appendix 1.

CHAPTER V Educating about alcohol

Introduction

The size and nature of the problem of alcohol misuse is such that the health and social services available can cope with only part of it. The primary objective, therefore, must be prevention. The aim of prevention is to influence people to form or to change their habits in a way which will lead to better health. Health education is an essential tool in this task, and this chapter looks at the nature of the educational message. How can it best be presented? And by whom?

The first task in health education is to convince people in general that this is an issue of importance; to arouse public awareness and stimulate public discussion.

There are some parallels with the anti-cigarette smoking campaign but these should not be pushed too far. Cigarette smoking is always harmful to the smoker and should therefore be given up or, at the very least, curtailed. The message on drinking is more subtle, since for the majority of drinkers alcohol is harmless. It is the minority—ie the *misusers*—who can cause harm to themselves, and to others.

Some people believe the health educator should try to promote total abstention. This is no new idea. But as the Advisory Committee on Alcoholism noted, health education needs 'to command broad approval from society at large. This alone is a sufficient reason for rejecting abstention as an aim for any preventive strategy'. Of course the views of non-drinkers must be respected. But to attempt to persuade the population at large to join them would, in the Government's view, be neither realistic nor desirable.

Perhaps the major factor in determining the extent of alcohol misuse in any society which uses alcohol widely, is the prevailing set of attitudes to its use; where social controls on alcohol use are strong and where drunkenness is frowned upon alcohol is taken moderately and in appropriate circumstances, and the amount of problem drinkers tend to be low. Health education, in this context, is about the strengthening of social controls.

Some organisations, individuals and even Government—for example in

France—have urged that a yard-stick be laid down; this would indicate rule-of-thumb limits of consumption which, if exceeded would increase the risk of alcohol-related harm.

The report of the Special Committee of the Royal College of Psychiatrists recommended that health education 'should give clear information as to what constitutes safe or dangerous levels of drinking', and suggested an absolute upper daily limit of 4 pints of beer or 4 doubles of spirits or one standard size bottle of wine. This would be a clear and simple approach and one that has been tried in France. There are drawbacks, however:

> Precise limits are not necessarily appropriate since, as has been shown, the effect of a given quantity of alcohol will vary considerably with the circumstances; whether taken with a meal or on an empty stomach and depending on the drinker's age, sex, weight and general reaction to alcohol.

> Limits would vary for different purposes. A consumption level set with a view to avoiding liver cirrhosis, even in the long-term, might well be sufficient to result in an immediate accident.

> There might be a tendency for some moderate drinkers to increase their intake 'up to the (dangerous) limit'.

The Royal College of Psychiatrists' report noted that its own suggested upper limits did not apply to drinking and driving and that, in any event, it would be most unwise to drink up to such levels habitually. A health education message, then, that recommended 'safe limits' might be counter-productive if it seemed to confer official approval on drinking levels which were in fact quite high.

The view of the Advisory Committee on Alcoholism was that health education should aim to encourage:

moderation in drinking;

drinking only in appropriate circumstances;

disapproval of inebriety;

and acceptance of abstention.

This approach would leave the onus of decision firmly on the individual drinker and would not enable him or her to shelter behind 'authoritative' advice on how much it was safe or sensible to drink. To be successful, a message in these terms would have to get through to ordinary social drinkers and persuade them to examine their own drinking habits and to consider whether these were potentially harmful to themselves or to others. Health education will not work if it is seen only as applying to someone else. The Advisory Committee recognised that encouragement of a favourable social climate—

one that frowned on misuse and accepted moderate drinking and abstention—would help individuals in making responsible decisions on the use of
alcohol. Indeed, an important aim of health education should be to oppose
attitudes to drinking that tend towards misuse. In the words of the Clayson
Report on Licensing in Scotland: 'If even a modest change can be made in the
public attitude towards drunkenness, so that 'hard drinking' is no longer a
symbol of manliness or the drunk an object of amused tolerance, the result
would pay an ample dividend on the cost of the (health education)
programme'.

Health education in schools
To be successful, health education must have a lasting effect on people's
behaviour. A long-term objective of this kind is more likely to be achieved if
health education 'catches people young' when they are more responsive to
persuasion and have less entrenched attitudes. The natural starting point for
formal health education for young people would seem to be the school.

When considering health education in schools, however, certain limitations need to be kept in mind:

The school is only one of a number of influences on the child. The home
environment is almost certainly the major factor in shaping the young
child's attitudes to alcohol, as to many other matters; though the media
and, later, ideas prevalent in the youngster's own age group also exert their
pressures.

The parents themselves are part of a large society. As is pointed out by the
report 'Health Education in Schools in Scotland'' (SED 1979) among
others, 'schools cannot be expected to embody, or create, a consensus of
health attitudes and behaviour when there is none in society'. If the school
tries to run quite counter to what is taught—perhaps by example—by the
parents, its action is likely to be ineffective; only when society itself alters
its fundamental attitudes to the use and misuse of alcohol can the school
exert its full influence.

A place must be found for such education within the school curriculum.

Most educationalists think it best to present health education as part of a
broad programme rather than as a specific subject on its own. In this way,
alcohol misuse is often included in a general programme designed to increase,
in the pupil, awareness of his or her own responsibility for his or her health
and well-being. This approach aims to help children to reach sensible
decisions for themselves. Such programmes would cover a range of issues
including use and misuse of alcohol, of tobacco and of drugs; sex education;
diet; hygiene and exercise. Presentation would develop through the school

years, from factual statements for younger children to a more sophisticated approach to adolescents.

As indicated, the responsibility for determining the school curriculum, lies formally with local education authorities and school governors; but it is, in practice, often delegated to head teachers. A difficult choice facing them is deciding how much time to allocate to health education. HM Inspectors of Schools do, however, offer advice and encourage schools to consider the adequacy of their health education work and their general approach to the subject; they do this by courses and visits to schools, and by stimulating interest in the organisations and projects mentioned below, and in DES publications such as 'Health Education in Schools', which contain advice on alcohol use and misuse. Voluntary organisations, such as the Teachers' Advisory Council on Alcohol and Drugs Education (TACADE), also help to train and equip teachers to teach health education. The Schools Council, the Health Education Council and the Scottish Health Education Group continue to sponsor curriculum developments and other projects on health education for schools and to disseminate the results.

General health education
Health education on alcohol misuse for the general population is essential, both for its own sake and because, as explained above, the teachers' efforts in schools will be nullified if there are conflicting attitudes between the home and the school. The Expenditure Committee, the Advisory Committee on Alcoholism and the Special Committee of the Royal College of Psychiatrists all advocated a greater effort through health education to warn people of the dangers of alcohol misuse and to encourage sensible attitudes towards drink.

At national level primary responsibility for health education lies, in England, Wales and Northern Ireland, with the Health Education Council (HEC) and, in Scotland, with the Scottish Health Education Group (SHEG). Since November 1977, the HEC, in conjunction with the North East Council on Alcoholism, has been running a pilot campaign in North East England to increase awareness of the effects of alcohol misuse and to encourage more responsible attitudes. This campaign which has recently included advice on sensible levels of consumption is being monitored, but it is too early to say whether it is proving effective. The experience gained in the North East will, however, help to determine the likely effectiveness of more widespread campaigns. The SHEG has mounted similar campaigns to help people to recognise the signs of alcohol misuse, to know about the agencies which can help and where to find them, and to reduce the stigma attached to alcoholism.

It is always difficult to gauge exactly the effectiveness of health education—and this is no less true in respect of alcohol misuse. Efforts to modify deeply entrenched attitudes and customs, such as those surrounding drinking, will produce results, if at all, only in the long-term. Furthermore, the effects of health education may be difficult to separate from other factors, such as change in price or availability.

While cigaratte smoking is far from analogous with misuse of alcohol, the long established anti-smoking campaign may nonetheless give an indication of the general effectiveness of health education. That campaign is believed to have contributed to the reduction from over 60% to 42% between 1960 and 1980 in the proportion of adult males in the United Kingdom who smoked cigarettes. (Over the same period, the proportion of women who smoke showed relatively little change.) In each year since 1973, the number of cigarettes sold has fallen and there has been a marked shift towards cigarettes with a lower tar yield. In the smoking field, then, measurable behaviour change has been observed.

Some people argue that health education messages are often swamped by countervailing commercial advertising and other influences; they compare the total measurable expenditure on alcohol education with spending on alcohol advertising. They point also to the strong influence, on young people especially, of behaviour portrayed on television and radio, and in books, plays and films where the presentation of drinking may be unbalanced.

Proponents of health education accept the strength of these other forces, but argue that campaigns on alcohol misuse will be effective if, as the Advisory Committee on Alcoholism put it, they are 'supported by a Government policy to maintain the existing control on availability of alcohol . . . . . and to maintain the price of alcohol in real terms' and if 'the presentation of alcohol to society . . . . . is modified to produce a less one-sided picture of its effects'. Opinions may differ on the degree of impact of health education on alcohol misuse but there is general agreement that its effectiveness will depend to a large extent on whether other forces are in concert with or in opposition to it.

Both the HEC and the SHEG are largely financed from general taxation by central government, though they are independent in their day-to-day operations. The budgets of both of these bodies have been significantly increased in recent years, but there are many calls on this money apart from programmes on the misuse of alcohol. Because of the high costs of alcohol misuse, an investment in health education now might pay rich dividends in the future. But the effects of health education are likely to be long-term and cumulative, whereas its costs through media campaigns are immediate and substantial.

'Care in Action' (1981), the DHSS handbook of policies and priorities for the Health and Personal Social Services in England, recognised not only the role of the HEC in health education, but also those of health authorities—whose strategies should include supporting the education authority in health education in schools on key topics, including alcohol use; and community physicians, other doctors, health visitors, nurses, midwives, organisers of voluntary services, social workers, teachers, and other paid and voluntary workers in the health, social services, and education fields. 'The Problem Drinker at Work' (1981), prepared jointly by the Health and Safety Executive, the Health Departments, and the Department of Employment, provides further advice on how firms can inform and educate employees about the dangers of alcohol misuse, as well as providing guidance on the joint role management and trade unions can play in assisting problem drinkers.

With support from the Government, the Licensing (Alcohol Education and Research) Act became law in 1981. The Act provides for the winding-up of the funds of the licensing compensation authorities (which were set up in England and Wales in 1904 to compensate publicans who lost their licences as a result of official action to reduce the number of alcohol outlets), and for half of the money in the funds (£4,300,000 in 1981) to be allocated to a trust fund known as the Alcohol Education and Research Fund which will be administered by a Council appointed by the Home Secretary. The money in the Fund is to be used primarily to educate the public about the causes and effects of alcohol misuse and to promote research into the means of preventing it. The Government is encouraged by the interest shown by the drinks industry in the establishment of the Council and by their intention of contributing additional funds for the Council's use. Several trade associations have already contributed to the production of health education material, as well as financing research into problem drinking. It is hoped that the Council will provide a new focus for health education in this field, and that its efforts will complement those being undertaken with Government support by the other bodies already mentioned.

The depiction of alcohol use in the media
Health education about alcohol is a positive attempt to warn people of the dangers of misuse and to persuade those who drink to do so sensibly. But, as we have just seen, some people believe that the influence of health education can be undermined if other persuasive forces—notably commercial advertising and the portrayal of drinking in the media—are not used responsibly.

Advertising
Views differ on the effects advertising has on the consumption of alcohol. The drinks industry itself maintains that its promotions influence the market

shares of particular brands rather than overall demand. Others believe that the cumulative effect of brand advertising must increase the overall demand for alcohol, especially amongst impressionable groups such as the young. It has also been argued that whether or not the volume of advertising leads to increased drinking, the contents of advertising may result in harmful patterns of consumption.

The Expenditure Committee, the Special Committee of the Royal College of Psychiatrists, and the Advisory Committee on Alcoholism all gave careful consideration to alcohol advertising. The former made no recommendation but, while expressing concern about the 'constant depiction of alcohol in advertisements as essential to success in life', . . . concluded that the dangers of alcohol advertising 'were not so readily apparent as to justify the limitation upon the range of products available to the moderate consumer' likely to result from a ban on such advertising. The Royal College of Psychiatrists thought that it would be surprising if alcohol advertising did not in some way augment pressures to drink, but recognised 'the dangers of too much State interference based on too little evidence', and recommended Government-commissioned research into the impact of liquor advertising. The DHSS Homelessness and Addictions Research Liaison Group has since published its strategy under which consideration will be given to research proposals submitted for funding in this field.* The Advisory Committee favoured encouragement of alcohol advertising which aimed to reinforce social controls against misuse.

At present, all broadcast advertising and most advertising in other media is subject to controls contained in codes of advertising practice. In the case of broadcast advertising, the Independent Broadcasting Authority (IBA) has a statutory duty to maintain and keep under review a code of advertising standards of practice, and it checks advertisements before transmission to ensure their compliance with the code's provisions. A section of the code relates to alcohol advertising, and it is kept under review by the IBA's Advertising Advisory Committee, upon which there is strong consumer and medical representation. On the Committee's recommendation, and in con-sultation with Government, these provisions were appreciably strengthened in October 1978. In addition, the independent television companies have voluntarily adopted a policy of not accepting advertisements for hard liquor.

Drink advertisements in most other media come under the alcohol provisions of the British Code of Advertising Practice which is administered by the Advertising Standards Authority (ASA). These provisions represent a

---

* See Appendix 3

form of self-regulation by the drinks industry itself, and a revised code, on which, once again, the Government was consulted, came into operation at the beginning of 1980. The ASA does not generally scrutinise advertisements in advance, but a recent survey by the Office of Fair Trading into the effectiveness of the ASA system did not find any alcohol advertisements that failed to meet the Code.

Under both codes, advertisements may not, for example, encourage excessive drinking; may not be directed specifically at the young; may not link drinking with driving; and may not make unrealistic claims about the benefits of alcohol. Through observation of these codes by advertisers and the drinks industry, the tone and content of alcohol advertising has changed considerably over the past 10 years.

Whether these arrangements and the current codes provide effective safeguards is still a matter for debate. The Government believes that there is scope for encouraging advertisers to consider how social controls against alcohol misuse could be more positively reinforced by advertisements. This could be a fruitful area for closer co-operation between Government and the drinks industry. It has been suggested, for example, that such advertisements might stress that the product was most enjoyable when taken in moderation, perhaps as an accompaniment to meals, and might usefully warn against such obvious misuses as drinking and driving. There has been some response to these suggestions and the Government intends to continue to keep in touch with representatives of the industry to see what more can be done.

The Government does not consider that legal restrictions or a ban on the advertising of alcohol would be justified by the research evidence available. To restrict expenditure on advertising might, in any case, simply release funds for other forms of promotion such as the sponsorship of sporting and other events. A total ban on advertising would be difficult to justify because unlike cigarettes—banned from TV advertising since 1965—alcohol, of itself, is not generally harmful to consumers. A ban solely on TV advertising, as some have suggested, would probably lead only to greater advertising efforts by other, and possibly no less effective, means.

Other media presentation

While there has been some research into the effects of advertising on alcohol sales, less is known about the subtle effects of the presentation of alcohol use in the media. But it would not be surprising if the depiction of drinking during TV and radio programmes, in plays, in books and in films were a stronger influence on people's behaviour than commercial advertising sponsored by obviously interested parties. The importance of media presentation was recognised by the Advisory Committee on Alcoholism who thought that it 'hardly ever shows that alcohol impairs and often contributes to accidents at work, at home, or on the road' and recommended that 'the presentation of alcohol to society should be modified to produce a less one-sided picture of its effects'. When alcohol *is* shown as causing impairment this is sometimes regarded as a subject for humour, while a large capacity for drink may be depicted as a sign of manliness.

Broadcasting has an educational as well as an entertainment function. The Advisory Committee suggested that 'long-running radio and television serials could be especially useful in illustrating the dangers of alcohol misuse'. Some of the major long-running series, for example 'The Archers' on the radio, and 'Coronation Street' on TV have in fact, drawn attention to the consequences of alcohol misuse. The BBC and the independent television companies have also broadcast in recent years a number of documentaries and other programmes dealing specifically with the alcohol misuse problem. Local radio too has played its part. Health education messages may be broadcast as well in the free public service time made available by the BBC and ITV companies.

Sensible drinking can be encouraged through health education responsibly reinforced in advertising and the media. Health education, even in this broader sense, cannot be relied on alone if strong forces continue to pull in other directions. A co-ordinated approach is necessary: one which not only involves all who are able through advertising and the media to help shape public attitudes, but also ensures that health and social implications are properly weighed in the consideration of legislative and fiscal policies, and recruits the efforts of those who come into contact socially or professionally with individuals at risk of developing drinking problems. The factors involved are examined in the next 3 chapters.

CHAPTER VI The law

Introduction

The law has long been used to penalise various kinds of anti-social acts resulting directly from misuse of alcohol. These range from simple drunkenness to more serious acts such as drinking and driving. It is also used to regulate the supply and consumption of alcohol. Regulation primarily takes the form of a system of licensing retail outlets but there are also specific prohibitions, particularly in respect of minimum age limits, and sanctions to ensure compliance.

The creation of specific offences will have some different effect on anti-social conduct but one which is not always easily calculable. The licensing system, however, and its related controls, represents a much broader preventive approach primarily aimed at moderating overall levels of consumption. It is undoubtedly effective to a certain extent in achieving this aim but there are difficulties in using it as a very precise means of reducing various forms of misuse. First, the licensing laws themselves can exert little direct control over drinking at home, of which there is increasing evidence. Second, they are effective in reducing misuse only insofar as misuse is directly related to overall levels of consumption. Finally, as many of the controls cannot be related specifically to particular forms of misuse and appear somewhat arbitrary their imposition has to be handled with care. The public will accept what it considers to be a reasonable degree of regulation. Regulation beyond that may lead only to widespread disregard of the law, to the reluctance of juries to convict, and to difficulties of enforcement. It is against this background that the licensing system, and possible changes in it have to be considered.

Preventive controls—licensing

Controls on availability

The system of regulating the retail sale and supply of alcohol broadly ensures that alcohol may not be retailed or supplied to the public without some form of prior authorisation. In premises where alcohol is sold by retail this takes the form of a licence granted by a local licensing authority and which specifies the premises in which sales may take place, whether for consumption 'on' or 'off' the premises. The licensing law also contains provisions for the sale or supply of drink in other establishments, such as members' clubs and canteens, where the supervising authorities and forms of authorisation are different but broadly comparable with the licensing system.

During the present century, significant changes have occurred in the provision of retail outlets. These are illustrated for England and Wales in the following tables.

Table 1: Number of outlets authorised to retail/supply intoxicating liquor

Outlet	1905	1945	1980
On-licences	99,478	72,960	90,802
Registered clubs	6,589*	15,590	26,889
Off-licences	25,405	21,599	37,252
Total outlets	131,472	110,149	154,943

Table 2: Table 1 expressed proportionately per 10,000 of population

Outlet	1905	1945	1980
On-licences	29.27	19.12	18.46
Registered clubs	1.94*	4.08	5.47
Off-licences	7.47	5.66	7.58
Total outlets	38.68	28.86	31.51
Total population (millions)	34	42.6	49.2

Source: Home Office Liquor Licensing Statistics for England and Wales.

* The figures for registered clubs in 1905 include also proprietary licensed clubs.

It will be seen from these tables that, although the total number of outlets has increased by about 17% since 1905, relative to the size of population there has been a decrease of about 18%. Although the total number of places where people drink on the premises (on-licences and registered clubs) has increased by about 11% in this period, relative to the size of the population there has been a decrease of some 33%. The number of public houses has remained fairly static since 1970 (fluctuating between 6.4 and 6.7 thousand). The number of licences granted to restaurants and residential establishments, however, has doubled in that period (from 10,300 in 1970 to 20,600 in 1980).

The substantial decrease in the number of on-licensed premises between 1905 and 1946 can be attributed largely to population redistribution and the tight control exercised by the licensing authorities over the grant of new licenses for public houses. There was a further contributory factor in England and Wales where, prior to the Licensing Act 1904, the licensing authority had only a very restricted power to refuse to renew licences. The 1904 Act relaxed those restrictions and, in the case of licences originally granted before the Act, gave the authorities power, subject to payment of compensation (see page 36), to refuse renewal on grounds including the over-provision of licences in the locality. Factors which seem likely to have contributed to the increase in recent years in the number of off-licences, (and the granting of off-licences to supermarkets and other food stores) are the changes made by the 1961 Licensing Act, which for the first time allowed off-licences to remain open during normal shop hours and reintroduced a right of appeal against magistrates' decisions. The abolition of resale price maintenance in 1964 has been an additional factor. The trends in Scotland and Northern Ireland have been similar to those in England and Wales.

Effectiveness of such controls
Experience here and in other countries suggests that controls on availability are capable of bringing about, at least, a measure of regulation of both the level of alcohol consumption and some forms of directly related harm. To take the extreme case, the introduction of prohibition in the United States of America initially reduced alcohol consumption and problems to the lowest recorded level. The opposite effects can be illustrated from Finland. When very tight alcohol controls were relaxed there in 1969, to permit the widespread establishment of medium-beer outlets, consumption of beer per head rose sharply, spirits consumption unexpectedly also increased and the number of heavy drinkers rose by 50% over the number in 1961. The limitations on regulation, in extreme form, however, are demonstrated by the fact that in the USA the level of consumption under prohibition later recovered to some extent as a result of the establishment of an illegal trade.

Concern about the effect of drunkenness on the war effort led to the establishment in 1915 of a Central Control Board, which imposed wideranging restrictions on alcohol consumption in areas where drunkenness was rife. Many of that Board's measures, including a sharp reduction in the previously permitted hours of $19\frac{1}{2}$ per weekday, and the prohibition of credit sales of alcohol, were retained after the war and still form the basis of our licensing laws. The implementation of the Board's measures was followed by a marked decline in both alcohol consumption and harm. Between 1914 and 1918 consumption of spirits halved and that of beer fell by almost two-thirds.

Between 1915 and 1918 drunkenness convictions decreased by 79%. But other factors, such as patriotic exhortation during wartime to reduce drinking; the mobilisation of a large part of the adult male population; curtailment of social activity; and restrictions on the production, importation and strength of alcohol, make it difficult to isolate and assess the effect of the Board's licensing restrictions. Comparisons of drunkenness and cirrhosis death rates between Board and non-Board areas in the early stages of the Board's activities does, however, suggest that the licensing restrictions initially brought about a sharp reduction in both phenomena. However, as other factors came into play and Board areas were extended, the effect of licensing restrictions became less directly apparent.

How constant the effect of regulation may be over a longer period, however, or how far it can be used to achieve precise or consistent results is less clear. Scotland and North East England both have above average consumption per head of alcohol, but, proportional to population, below average numbers of licensed outlets. Moreover, until 1976, permitted hours in Scotland, where the alcohol misuse problem has always been particularly acute, were appreciably more restricted than those in England and Wales.

Available evidence therefore suggests that licensing restrictions may have a broad influence on both the level of average consumption per head of alcohol and the incidence of alcohol-related harm, but that minor changes or variations in such restrictions may have little effect by themselves. The matter is one which is commented on specifically by a Departmental Committee set up to review the Liquor Licensing Laws in Scotland under the chairmanship of Dr Christopher Clayson. In its report, published in 1973, the Committee reached the conclusion, in relation to the comparatively minor changes proposed to them that 'licensing, a negative and restrictive process, can only play a strictly limited part in the control of alcohol misuse'.

The Report also suggests that the most important consequences of licensing restrictions may be their effect on drinking *patterns*. Many factors influence alcohol consumption, but licensing laws exert a unique control over when and where people drink. The 'afternoon break' in particular was introduced for the purpose of preventing day-long drinking sessions. Some Scottish licensing authorities have recently used the wider powers to grant extensions they were given under the Licensing (Scotland) Act 1976 to permit opening throughout the afternoon hours. The effect of such extensions cannot yet be measured.

Evidence of the influence of licensing hours and consumption patterns comes from Victoria, Australia, where a study of the effect on motor accidents of a change in closing time from 6 pm to 10 pm found that, although the overall total of personal injury accidents remained unchanged, the previous accident peak between 6 and 7 pm had disappeared and had been replaced by one between 10 and 11 pm. It is accordingly possible that changes in licensing hours had significantly affected drinking patterns without apparently influencing overall consumption levels.

Possible changes in controls on availability
A Departmental Committee was set up in 1970 under Lord Erroll of Hale to review the liquor laws in England and Wales. The Committee formed the view that

> the absolute powers of the licensing magistrates led to inconsistencies in practice;
>
> magistrates should not be concerned with the market demand for proposed new outlets;
>
> the licensing system should be more flexible to cater for changes in leisure habits and consumer demand.

This last view is also held by organisations in the tourist industry, who believe that some foreign tourists may find Britain less attractive to visit because of (to them) restrictive licensing hours. In its Report, published in 1972, the Committee accordingly made various recommendations which in total would have somewhat relaxed the licensing laws. These included

> limiting licensing magistrates' power to refuse an on- or off-licence to specified grounds;
>
> a considerable extension for permitted hours for on-licences;
>
> power for licensing magistrates to waive permitted hours restrictions for restaurants and places of entertainment where the sale of liquor is ancillary to other activities.

No decisions have been taken on these recommendations of the Erroll Committee. The Government of the day did not accept the comparable Clayson Committee recommendation that the number of outlets in Scotland should be left to commercial forces, and the Licensing (Scotland) Act 1976 retains the power to refuse a licence on the grounds that its grant would result in over-provision in the locality.

Since the Erroll Committee reported, a trend has become clear, starting from about 1970, of a sharp increase in alcohol-related harm which has resulted in opposition to its proposals for relaxation. There is no clear evidence of the effect of changes in licensing laws. In Scotland, where the laws were previously more restrictive than in England and Wales, there are indications that the extended permitted hours and the Sunday opening of many public houses following on the Clayson Report have not resulted in any increase in total consumption. The change in the evening closing hours from

10 pm to 11 pm appears significantly to have reduced heavy drinking 'against the clock in the final hour'. But it would be unwise to draw any general conclusion from the early effects of such minor relaxations in one country or to suggest that other relaxations would not have a harmful effect. The present Government has made it clear that it has no plans to amend the licensing laws of England and Wales in the light of the more controversial recommendations of the Erroll Committee Report.

The sharp increase in alcohol-related harm in recent years might suggest that our licensing laws ought, if anything, to be tightened. However the Expenditure Committee and the Advisory Committee on Alcoholism both took the view that, although extreme caution should be taken over any possible relaxation, there was no case for tightening present restrictions. Similar views were expressed in the report of the Special Committee of the Royal College of Psychiatrists and in the Report on liquor licensing in Northern Ireland.

Minimum age limits

The legal provisions regulating a supply of alcohol to young people provide, broadly, that children under 5 may not be given non-medicinal alcohol in any circumstances; that those under 14 (18 in Northern Ireland) may not enter bars; and that those under 18 may not be sold or supplied with and may not attempt to purchase, alcohol in a bar or off-licence. It is not unlawful for people under 18 to possess or consume alcoholic drinks either in private or (except in a licensed bar) in public; and (except in Northern Ireland) young people over 16 may, for consumption with a meal away from a bar, buy beer, cider or perry, and in Scotland may, in addition, buy wine, with meals so taken.

Under the Licensing Acts it is an offence for a licensee knowingly to sell intoxicating liquor to young people under 18, or to allow them to drink in a bar. Young people under 18 are also liable to prosecution if they drink alcohol in a bar. The enforcement of the law relating to under-age drinking provides difficulties for the police and publicans alike, but it is for them to determine locally how best this is done. Because it is often so difficult—particularly at times when trade is busy—for publicans and their staff to ensure that customers are above the legal age, it has occasionally been suggested that young people should be required to produce identity cards on demand to prove that they are over 18. This proposal has been reiterated recently in a document submitted to the Government by the National Union of Licensed Victuallers ('The Case for Change') in association with a proposal to reduce the minimum drinking age to 16. The Erroll Committee did in fact consider this suggestion but rejected it as unworkable, and unacceptable to public opinion at large. There is nothing to prevent people voluntarily carrying identification cards but the Government shares the view of the Erroll Committee that a legally enforceable requirement to carry a card would not be acceptable.

Effectiveness of age limits

The sale of alcohol to young people has been legally restricted in this country since 1872; the present 18 years limit was introduced in 1923. The case for age restrictions is based on the widespread belief that young people should not be exposed on their own to the risks of alcohol until they are old enough to recognise its potency and use it widely. But current age limits seem to be widely flouted in practice. Fifteen per cent of 13-16 year olds, and 35% of the 17 year olds, in Hawker's study on adolescence and alcohol reported that they usually drank in public houses. These findings and the sharp rise in such indicators as the number of young people found guilty of drunkenness offences (Figure 3), may suggest that the law on age limits is becoming increasingly ineffective. In a society where independence is reached at an earlier age than in the past, there is the related problem that in many areas insufficient attractive, alternative venues exist where teenagers can meet and relax away from their homes.

The authors of a study of youths between 14 and 17 in Glasgow, referred to in Chapter IV, found that drinking was widespread and that, when drinking outside the home, the younger teenagers mainly drank in the open air or secretly in dance halls while the older teenagers in the sample drank predominantly in public houses. They considered the prohibition on consumption under 18 in a bar and concluded that it dictated only *where* rather than *whether* young people drank. They suggested that, rather than have young teenagers drinking secretly, 'it might be worthwhile considering whether they should be permitted to drink under adult supervision in the public house'.

The Erroll Committee formed the view that a reduction of the age limit to 17 years would recognise social realities and marginally assist law enforcement; and that allowing young children into suitable bars would, by encouraging the development of family facilities, be socially advantageous. Seventeen year olds, the Committee thought, were no more prone to excessive drinking than 18 year olds. They accordingly recommended some relaxation of the age limits, including a reduction of the 18 year age limit to 17 years and giving licensing magistrates a new power to authorise admission of children under 14 to bars in suitable licensed premises.

The marked increase in alcohol-related harm suffered by young people since the Erroll Committee reported, however, has led all the bodies which have considered this question in recent years to recommend against any age limit relaxations. The Advisory Committee on Alcoholism drew attention to experiences in the USA where several States had, in recent years, reduced the age limit from 21 to 18. Subsequent studies there had shown a substantial increase in alcohol consumption by 18-20 year olds and an associated increase in alcohol-related road accidents in that age group. Other evidence from the USA similarly indicated that the lowering of age limits leads generally to increased alcohol consumption and harm among young people. The Expenditure Committee recommended that 'the age at which alcohol is made legally available should in no circumstances be lowered'. The Clayson Committee on Scottish licensing law, the Special Committee of the Royal College of Psychiatrists and the Inter-Departmental Review Body on Liquor in Northern Ireland also found no case for a lowering of the age. A Clayson Committee recommendation, similar to that of the Erroll Committee, that children under 14 should be permitted in suitable bars was rejected by the Government of the day.

Occupational Regulatory laws
Anyone under the influence of drink at work who thereby endangers the health and safety of himself or others is liable to prosecution under the provision of Section 7 of the Health and Safety at Work etc Act 1974 (Article 8 of the Health and Safety at Work (Northern Ireland) Order 1978).* Other statutory provisions make drunkenness on duty an offence by railwaymen (Railway Regulations Act 1842; and British Railways Board Bye-law 16) and postmen (Post Office Act 1953) and make it an offence to drink alcohol while working in compressed air (Work in Compressed Air Special Regulations 1958 and Work in Compressed Air Special Regulations (Northern Ireland) 1963).

Additional legal restrictions govern the use of alcohol by those in certain occupations such as pilots and seamen. It is an offence under the Air Navigation Order 1980 for civil pilots to act as crew members if their capacity to carry out their duties is impaired by alcohol. Controls exercised by the Civil Aviation Authority prohibit the consumption of alcohol by a pilot for at least 8 hours before flying. Offenders are liable to a maximum fine of £400 and/or

---

* Footnote: The Act and Order place a duty on every employee while at work to take reasonable care for the health and safety of himself and of other people who may be affected by his acts or omissions at his work. Employers who fail to take adequate steps to deal with such behaviour could be held to be in breach of Section 2 of the Act (Article 4 of the Order) which places a duty on employers to ensure so far as is reasonably practicable the health, safety and welfare at work of their employees.

imprisonment for a maximum of 2 years. Under the Merchant Shipping Acts, in recognition of the particular problem, criminal sanctions are provided against any seafarer serving on a United Kingdom registered vessel whose actions or failure to act whilst under the influence of drink contribute towards serious material damage or to the death of or serious injury to any person on board. Possession of alcohol aboard United Kingdom registered fishing vessels will be closely regulated, and made subject to inspection when Section 25 of the Merchant Shipping Act 1979 comes into force.

New regulatory laws

As a measure against football hooliganism, new laws were introduced in Scotland in 1980 to prohibit drink at major soccer and rugby matches and in buses taking supporters to matches. Under the Transport Act 1980, regulations have been made which give the Traffic Commissioners statutory powers to attach conditions to public service vehicles' licences restricting the carriage of drink on football excursions. British Rail have also introduced a byelaw which enables them to prohibit the carriage and consumption of drink on specified trains. The early effects of these measures have been generally judged to be satisfactory. Possibly there is a case for prohibitions or restrictions on alcohol on other occasions where intoxication appears to contribute to a particular risk of violence or offensive conduct.

Deterrent laws

Alcohol may play a part in many types of crime but there are 2 main areas—public drunkenness and drinking and drinking and driving—where alcohol misuse is itself an offence. The questions now to be looked at are whether the law provides an adequate deterrent in those areas, and whether it could be used to deter other forms of misuse.

Drunkenness offences

In England and Wales these offences comprise simple drunkenness (being found drunk in a highway or other public place) and drunkenness with aggravation (for example, being drunk and disorderly). The maximum penalties for these offences are fines of £25 and £50 respectively, although some 2-3% of offenders are subsequently committed to prison for non-payment of fine. Most prosecutions in England and Wales are brought under the Licensing Act 1872.

Being drunk and incapable is an offence in Scotland under the Licensing (Scotland) Act 1903, and the penalty of a fine was increased by the Criminal Justice (Scotland) Act 1980 from £5 to £50 maximum. Where the offender is already dependent on alcohol, these penal laws are recognised to be ineffec tive in preventing alcohol misuse and, as resources can be made available, experiments are being instituted in diverting habitual drunken offenders from the penal system into arrangements for treatment and care. The Criminal Justice (Scotland) Act 1980 makes special provision to help the habitual drunkard. But these long-standing laws may, nevertheless, have a deterrent effect for some ordinary social drinkers, and arrest by the police may well save some habitual drunkards from injuring themselves or others.

Drinking and driving

The drinking and driving laws and the penalties they carry might be expected to provide an effective deterrent. Loss of driving licence, which is likely to cause most people considerable inconvenience and may cost some their livelihood, ought to be an especially effective sanction. Nonetheless, as described in Chapter 3, although deaths from alcohol related traffic accidents were dramatically reduced after the 1967 Road Safety Act came into force, they increased steadily to a peak in 1976, and have now dropped back.

Concern about this trend led to the appointment in 1974 of the Blennerhassett Committee to look at the whole question of drinking and driving. On the blood alcohol limit, the Committee formed the view that better enforcement of the 80 mg/100 ml limit would be a more effective measure than lowering the limit as has been done in some countries. They saw real disadvantages in extending the category of potential offenders when in practice many offenders driving over the present limit avoided detection. To improve detection, the Committee felt that existing restrictions on breath-testing by the police should be removed. The Committee also considered whether stricter penalties for drinking and driving might help to reduce the number of offences, but concluded that disqualification for longer than the one year would tempt more people to drive while disqualified, and would in any event not be generally acceptable to public opinion.

In 1979 the Department of Transport issued a consultative document on the Blennerhassett proposals, and legislative changes were made to the Road Traffic Act 1972 in the Transport Act 1981. These will come into effect in late 1982. They will tighten up the law by closing a number of loopholes and will make it easier to enforce by introducing evidential breath analysis. However, the Government decided not to introduce 'random testing' because of the effect it would have on police/public relations. Plans are also being drawn up, using the existing law, to ensure that repeat offenders found to have excessive blood alcohol levels do not automatically regain their licences after disqualification if medical advice suggests that they have a drinking problem.

CHAPTER VII Tax and price disincentives

Introduction

It was suggested in Chapter IV that there may be a direct link between the level of alcohol consumption per head and the level of alcohol-related harm. If this is so, it would follow that measures to check the growth in consumption per head should also help to check the growth in harm. The level of consumption per head in any society will depend to a large extent on social and cultural influences. These and other factors which may affect alcohol consumption, including advertising and licensing restrictions, were examined in previous chapters. But in addition to these influences the demand for alcoholic drink will be affected by its price relative to the price of other goods and by the level of consumers' real disposable income per head. One element affecting the relative price of alcohol, which is directly under the Government's control, is taxation and the present chapter considers the implications of using this to influence the level of consumption.

Current Taxation

In common with tobacco and hydrocarbon oils, alcoholic drinks are currently subject to both excise duties and VAT at the standard rate of 15%. Table 3 shows that these taxes together account for a high proportion of the average price of most alcoholic drinks in the UK. The actual proportion, however, varies considerably from about a third in the case of beer and wine to over half in the case of spirits. (This relates to average prices of all sales, including those in bars and restaurants: for off-licence sales alone the tax will be a somewhat higher proportion of the retail price.) The excise duties together with VAT on alcoholic drinks are estimated to have raised around £4,000m in 1980-81 when they accounted for about 6% of central government revenue.

VAT is charged as a percentage of the net retail price, and thus responds automatically to price changes; but, in common with the practice in most Western countries and for most other commodities which are subject to excise duties, the excise duties on alcoholic drinks in the UK are fixed in money terms in relation to a given quantity (eg £95.20 per hectolitre for table wine). The real value of these specific duties becomes reduced by inflation, with the result that the tax-inclusive real price will tend to fall unless these duties are increased regularly in line with the rise in the general price level, or unless the basic tax-exclusive price of these goods rises at a faster rate than prices in general.

Table 3: Tax as a percentage of consumers' expenditure on alcoholic drink

	1968	1969	1970	1971	1972	1973	1974	1975	1976	1977	1978	1979
Beer	36.6	36.9	33.4	30.9	29.1	28.6	28.5	29.9	30.5	30.0	28.7	29.2
Spirits	56.3	57.9	56.2	54.6	53.5	52.2	53.5	52.8	58.1	53.5	53.7	52.7
Wines, Cider and Perry	23.2	26.3	26.4	28.2	24.4	22.9	24.2	29.1	31.0	31.0	30.7	31.5
All alcoholic drink	40.0	40.7	38.5	36.6	34.8	34.5	34.9	36.1	38.0	36.1	35.6	36.1

Source: 1980 Blue Book

NOTE: These figures relate to consumer expenditure in all outlets, including bars, hotels and restaurants, as well as off-licences, supermarkets and public houses. Since duty is charged in relation to quantity and alcoholic strength rather than price, in practice it will vary widely as a proportion of price. The figures given here indicate the proportion which tax represents for the average priced drink in each category.

The level of the specific duties is reviewed annually at the time of the Budget (although the Chancellor of the Exchequer is also empowered to change the duties at other times of the year by up to 10% under the 'Regulator' provisions). It is for the Chancellor to decide in the light of a wide range of factors, whether and by how much, the duties are altered.

Figure 5 shows that the real price of alcoholic drinks fell fairly steadily over the period 1970-79 as a whole. However, the increase in the standard rate of VAT in 1979 made alcohol taxation more responsive to changes in the price, and the specific duty increases in the 1981 Budget have resulted in some increase in the real price. For example, in the case of beer, the real value of the duty has been restored to close to its 1975 level.

Recent recommendations on prices and tax disincentives

Both the House of Commons Expenditure Committee and the Advisory Committee on Alcoholism published reports in 1977 recommending the maintenance of the price of alcohol in relation to incomes. The Expenditure Committee thought that '... the price of alcoholic drink should remain at the same level relative to average incomes as it now is ...', while the view of the Advisory Committee was that '... alcohol should not be allowed to become cheaper in real terms, and that when real income levels rise, taxation levels on

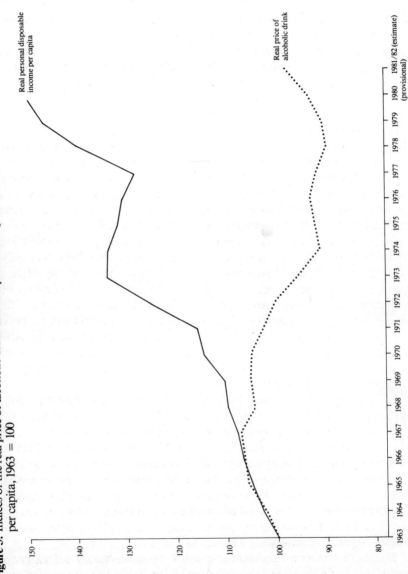

Figure 5. Indices of the real price of alcoholic drink and real personal disposal income per capita, 1963 = 100

alcohol should be adjusted to counteract the increased buoyancy of consumer spending'.

The Special Committee of the Royal College of Psychiatrists, in its 1979 Report on 'Alcohol and Alcoholism', went further in recommending that '... public revenue policies of Government should be intentionally employed in the interests of health, so as to ensure that per capita alcohol consumption does not increase beyond the present level, and is by stages brought to an agreed lower level ...'. The report recognises that the level to which consumption should be reduced would be a matter for consultation and public debate, but suggested that one goal might be to reduce consumption over the next 10 years to the level it was a decade ago.

Effectiveness of the use of taxation as a disincentive

These recommendations were based on the premise that where in a given society consumption of alcohol increases per head, this is principally as a result of drinkers at all levels raising their intake, rather than of non-drinkers taking to alcohol for the first time. It is argued that maintaining the real price of alcohol in line with increases in prices generally, and still more increasing the real price of alcohol, might deter people from drinking more and so protect some of them from harm. It might be successful also in restraining some of those who misuse alcohol periodically rather than persistently. But maintaining or increasing the real price of alcohol is not likely to influence many problem drinkers who will probably maintain their consumption by switching to a cheaper drink or reducing their expenditure on other items—perhaps to the detriment of their family. This suggests that increasing the real price of alcohol by increased taxation could play only a limited part in dealing with the problem of alcohol misuse. It is unlikely that it would discourage the highly dependent, but it might encourage others to keep their drinking within safer limits.

But the possible use of taxation as a disincentive to increasing the number of problem drinkers would necessarily be a blunt instrument which would affect those who did not need protection as much as those who did. With the taxation instruments available, it would not be possible to treat individuals differently; nor is there any objective evidence to suggest that consumption of any one type of alcoholic drink should be encouraged at the expense of another because it is less likely to lead to misuse. This inevitably raises the question of how far it is justified to take measures that would restrict—or increase the cost of the enjoyment of the great majority in order to check misuse or potential misuse by a minority.

Moreover, increases in alcoholic drink taxation would affect people differently not only according to their drinking habits but also according to their level of income. As Table 4 shows, expenditure on wine and spirits generally forms a higher proportion of total expenditure as total income increases. Expenditure on beer is at its highest proportionately in the middle incomes, and thereafter declines as a proportion of income as income increases. The Table suggests that the impact of increased taxation overall, would be greater on those in the middle and higher income ranges, since households in those ranges spend a greater proportion of their income on alcoholic drinks.

The degree to which changes in the real burden of taxation on alcoholic drinks could be expected to affect the overall level of alcohol consumption would depend primarily on the sensitivity of the quantity of alcohol consumed to changes in its price compared with other goods. Consumption may also be influenced by social factors (such as changes in population and tastes) and by changes in real disposable income. ('Real disposable income' is the amount which consumers have available to spend after taking account of the rate of inflation and of statutory payments such as income tax.)

Evidence of a number of studies is that the sensitivity of demand to changes in relative prices and consumers' real disposable incomes, and to the influence of social factors, varies considerably between different types of alcoholic drink. The calculations also vary according to the nature of the assumption made about consumers' behaviour in the markets for alcoholic drink. For this reason it is not possible to produce absolutely firm estimates of how consumption would respond if, for example, the relative price of alcohol were deliberately raised by increasing the specific duties by more than the rate of inflation. The figures are subject to continuous revision as further information and evidence comes to light.

As an example, those relationships used as part of the Treasury Macro-economic model* and based on the analysis of past trends, assume that changes in the relative price of alcohol and in real disposable incomes are the main factors which produce changes in the volume consumed.

They additionally suggest that for a 1% rise in its relative price, consumer's demand for beer might be expected to fall by about $\frac{1}{4}$%. For spirits, the reduction in demand might be of the order of 1$\frac{1}{2}$% and for wine 1%. A 1% rise in real incomes, on the other hand, might be expected to increase consumers' demand for beer by about $\frac{1}{4}$%, for spirits by about 2$\frac{1}{4}$%, and for wine by about 2$\frac{1}{2}$%.** This in turn suggests that over the years consumption of beer has been less sensitive to both changes in price and income than wine and spir-

* HM Treasury Macroeconomic Model Equation and Variable Listing (May 1980 version). HM Treasury, Parliament Street, London SW1. See also 'The Change in Revenue from an Indirect Tax Change'. Economic Trends no 317 March 1980.

** For Further illustrations see Treasury Background Notes, 'A Tax Ready Reckoner' (Supplement to Economic Progress Report May 1981).

Table 4: Average weekly household expenditure on alcoholic drinks as a percentage of total weekly household expenditure on goods and service:

One man, one woman, 2 children households

Gross normal weekly income of household	Under £80	£ 80-£100	£100-£120	£120-£150	£150-£200	£200 or more	All house-holds
Beer, cider etc	2.6	3.1	2.5	2.9	2.4	1.6	2.5
Wine, spirits etc	0.9	0.5	0.7	1.1	1.2	2.1	1.3
Drink not defined	—	0.5	0.6	0.5	0.7	0.6	0.6
All alcoholic drink	3.6	4.1	3.8	4.5	4.3	4.3	4.3

One man, one woman, retired households, mainly dependent on state pensions

Gross normal weekly income	Under £40	£40-£45	£45 or more	All house-holds
Beer, cider etc	2.0	2.1	2.0	2.1
Wines, spirits etc	0.9	0.6	1.1	1.0
Drink not defined	—	[0.2]	—	[0.1]
All alcoholic drink	3.0	2.9	3.2	3.2

One adult, non-retired households

Gross normal weekly income	Under £30	£30-£45	£45-£60	£60-£75	£ 75-£100	£100 or more	All house-holds
Beer, cider etc	3.1	1.0	2.9	3.5	4.5	2.4	3.1
Wines, spirits etc	0.7	1.3	1.0	1.6	1.8	3.0	2.1
Drink not defined	—	—	(0.5)*	0.9	1.3	1.1	0.9
All alcoholic drink	4.0	2.4	4.4	6.0	7.6	6.5	6.1

One man, one woman, non-retired households

Gross normal weekly income of household	Under £60	£60-£80	£ 80-£100	£100-£120	£120-£140	£140-£160	£160-£200	£200 or more	All house-holds
Beer, cider etc	3.4	2.9	3.3	2.9	2.9	2.7	2.4	1.7	2.6
Wine, spirits etc	0.8	1.0	1.0	2.0	1.8	1.4	1.8	2.5	1.8
Drink not defined	(0.5)*	[0.3]	0.5	1.6	1.0	1.1	1.0	1.1	1.0
All alcoholic drink	4.8	4.2	4.9	6.5	5.8	5.2	5.2	5.3	5.3

All Households

	All households
Beer, cider etc	2.7
Wines, spirits etc	1.4
Drink not defined	0.7
All alcoholic drink	4.8

* Sampling error 50% or more
Source: 1979 FES

its, and that consumption of alcoholic drinks as a whole is on average less sensitive to rises in prices than to rises in disposable incomes.

Leaving aside the effects of social influences this points to the conclusion that the level of alcoholic consumption could be expected to increase during any period in which real incomes were rising, unless the real price of alcoholic drink increased by significantly more than incomes. Given that tax represents only part (although admittedly a considerable part) of the price to the consumer, the amount by which it might be necessary to alter the real burden of tax in order to achieve a particular consumption level would depend in part on how the relative tax-exclusive price of alcoholic drinks moved. But all these factors suggest that in a period when real incomes are rising, significant increases in the real tax burden on alcoholic drinks might be necessary if the objective was to prevent consumption rising, and that substantial increases would be needed if the aim were to reduce consumption.

It is also necessary to bear in mind the possibility that changes in the tax burden on particular alcoholic drinks may have a more immediate effect on the pattern of consumption than on its overall level. The difference between the demand relationships for beer and other alcoholic drinks described above, for instance, partly reflects the evidence that drinkers in part respond to increases in the overall price level of alcoholic drinks by switching to cheaper forms of alcohol including home-produced wine and beer; and at the extreme, if the price rose substantially and the demand for alcohol persisted, there could be an incentive for the illegal production and sale of alcoholic drink.

Economic implications

A further consideration in setting alcohol duties primarily to serve health and social ends is that this would reduce their value to the Government as flexible instruments for obtaining revenue and for wider economic policy. The extent of this reduction would depend on whether the Government adopted as its target simply the maintenance of the real value of the duties, or their adjustment in such a way as to maintain or reduce consumption of alcoholic drinks at a certain level.

The taxation of alcoholic drinks accounts for a significant proportion (6%) of central government revenue. Ceasing to vary the level of the duties primarily in accordance with the need for revenue or with the needs of the economy would mean that the revenue from a significant source might be either more or less than if the judgement were being made on grounds of economic policy. This could have implications for the levels of other taxes, either by pre- empting the capacity within the economy for maintaining or increasing the levels of other indirect taxes or—if consumption were reduced to such an extent that revenue fell—by requiring increases in other taxes if Government expenditure were not to be reduced or borrowing to rise. In either event this could have consequences for the Government's ability to take other factors (such as energy policy) into account in setting other indirect taxes.

Any approach which relied on deliberate increases in the level of duties on alcoholic drinks could not be operated without taking into account a number of other important questions of policy. The relative levels of the duties on different alcoholic drinks might not to be found to be appropriate at any particular time, and the power to adjust these relationships would need to be retained. Regard would also have to be paid to the overall effect of any changes on the Retail Price Index (RPI), which could influence future wage bargaining. And the Government would have to reserve to itself 'override powers' (of the kind already found in the legislation for the indexation of the income tax personal allowances and thresholds) to cancel or reduce duty increases in the light of wider economic factors to which greater priority had to be given.

If the policy objective were to adjust the duties so as to maintain or reduce consumption at a pre-determined level it would be necessary to take particularly into account the effect of changes in factor costs and of the underlying trends in the consumption of particular types of drink. This would be difficult to achieve at the time when adjustments were being made to the duty, and so it would be necessary to rely on a broad judgement as to the levels of duty which would hold consumption at the required level.

Any social, legal or fiscal measures to contain or reduce consumption could have adverse effects on the output, employment and investment of the drinks industries, on the activities of associated industries and (overall) on the economy generally which would need to be taken fully into account. It is difficult to quantify all these effects, particularly as they would obviously vary according to the targets set, the actual changes produced in the volume of particular drinks consumed, and on whether, and to what degree, the direct economic losses were offset by some transfer of expenditure by consumers to other goods and services (with a consequent expansion in those industries) and by some reduction in the economic costs associated with problem drinking.

The proportion of total consumers' expenditure attributable to beer, wine and spirits is about $7\frac{1}{2}\%$ or over one-quarter of consumers' expenditure on all food and drinks. Production of beer, malt and spirits account for a little more than 2% of total UK industrial activity, which is more than the proportion attributable to either the shipbuilding or the aerospace industries. Although most wine is imported, about 50% is bottled in the UK, including substantial quantities of fortified wines for export.

It is estimated that about 700,000 jobs in the UK are, to some extent, dependent on the alcohol industry and trade. About 100,000 people are directly employed in the production and bottling processes (about 1% of all those employed in production industries). A further 600,000 persons are employed in whole or in part in the sale and distribution of alcohol, in pubs, off-licences, hotels, clubs and restaurants (about 2½% of the total employed in industry and services). Finally, the supply of raw materials and other inputs to the alcoholic drinks industry generates further employment, particularly in the construction and related industries for whom the brewing and distilling are important customers (for capital investment alone, about £100 million at 1978 prices over the 3 years 1978-80 during a period of low investment generally).

As far as the UK balance of payments is concerned, total exports of alcoholic drinks in 1980 amounted to £880 million or 1.9% of the value of total exports, exports of spirits alone accounting for £830 million or 1.8%. Until recently there has been a regular and considerable annual increase in the value of exports of spirits. The present world-wide recession has slowed this trend but it is expected that as the world economy recovers the value of spirits exports will resume an upward trend.

The practical effects of any change in tax policies in particular in this direction would vary between the individual drinks industries. For example, in the case of beer, any fall in consumption would lead to a reduced use of capacity, increased unit costs and possibly some reduction in employment, and the relatively small export base would make it very unlikely that increased exports could compensate for any significant reduction in home consumption. In the case of spirits, exports and export prospects are usually more important to the Scotch Whisky industry than the home market. (At present over 80% of whisky is exported.) But (particularly because of the importance of the whisky industry to the economy of rural areas of Scotland), it has to be remembered that a reduction in home consumption could further affect the spirits industry at a time of world-wide recession when the industry is already suffering short- time working and redundancies. In particular, the average 6-year maturation period required, causes changes in consumption to have a quite disproportionate effect on immediate production requirements. During the summer of 1981, for example, these factors together resulted in the industry operating at only 30-60% capacity with significant employment effects at a time when consumption had fallen by only some 4%. In the case of wine, any reduction in consumption would be concentrated on the lower quality wines bottled in the UK, given that the duty represents a higher proportion of their price than of higher quality wines imported in bottles.

Taking account of the economic as well as the health and social considerations, and bearing in mind the practical difficulties involved, the Government cannot accept recommendations that have been made for the systematic use of tax rates as a means of regulating consumption. Health and social implications are, however, clearly of great importance, and the Government intends, within the context of its overall economic strategy, to continue to take these into account when changes in duty and wider taxation policy are considered.

CHAPTER VIII Early identification and help

Reason for why we will target young drinkers

Introduction

However effective measures may be to encourage people to drink sensibly, some individuals will still develop drinking problems and it is essential that they are helped to recognise their problems. The most effective step forward is early recognition by individuals of the need to curb misuse of alcohol and to control their problems before continued alcohol misuse endangers health, work prospects and family life. Equally important, however, is the influence of family and friends. Often they may recognise the signs of misuse before the individual and can, by their concern, stimulate self help.

A first requirement, therefore, is the education of the community on how misuse can occur and on the signs that it is occurring. Widespread publication of information on the effects of alcohol misuse will not only ensure that the public are better informed, but should help to strengthen individuals' resolve and willingness to identify and help people with problems at the earliest possible stage.

Intervention even at a later stage can help those with serious drinking problems and their families; but inevitably this will mean the investment of more time and resources. It is important to recognise that the later the intervention, the less is the the likelihood of effective help and support for problem drinkers from their families and friends, and the more the families themselves will need help with their problems.

Help at work

Many problem drinkers are in regular employment, and can be helped by companies which adopt policies for problem drinkers and encourage initiatives to help them while at work. Guidance on the way management and trade unions can act together to assist problem drinkers has been issued by the Health and Safety Executive in its publication 'The Problem Drinker at Work', prepared jointly with the Health Departments of Great Britain and the Department of Employment. Similar guidance has been issued in Northern Ireland.

Several employers, following the lead of firms in the drinks industry, have been operating policies to help employees who are misusing alcohol. The Government, too, as a major employer, is playing its part. Guidance which closely follows that in 'The Problem Drinker at Work', has been circulated to all Government Departments who will draw up their own policies in consultation with their trade unions to help staff with drinking problems. Some departments have already developed their arrangements. The Health Departments hope that health and local authorities, corporations and companies in the public as well as in the private sector will follow this example.

The guidance in 'The Problem Drinker at Work' should, if widely discussed and made available, help firms to adopt a more positive policy of encouraging employees with drinking problems to seek help without fear for their jobs. Employers and employees wishing to develop more positive alcohol policies can be helped by material provided from voluntary organisations such as the National Council on Alcoholism, the Scottish Council on Alcoholism and the Alcohol Education Centre, and in Northern Ireland from the Northern Ireland Council on Alcohol and the Council on Alcohol Related Problems.

Help from the Professions
There are many groups such as personnel and welfare officers, magistrates, police officers, teachers and many voluntary workers (for example the Samaritans) who, through their work may come into contact with people who have drinking problems. Often they are well placed to identify signs of alcohol misuse before these are recognised by the individuals themselves. Such groups are becoming increasingly alert to these signs and to the help they can give if their responses are geared more positively to encouraging individuals to control their drinking or to seek advice and assistance. Many people with incipient problems will respond to such a positive interest and the realisation that further misuse can cause themselves and others serious harm. There have been some important initiatives among these groups. The Magistrates' Association Juvenile Courts Committee, for example, has set up a Sub-Committee concerned with children and alcohol.

Certain other groups are probably more regularly in touch with problem drinkers and particularly well placed to identify alcohol misuse in its earlier stages. These include prison Medical Officers, social workers, probation officers, General Practitioners and other members of the primary health care team, and voluntary counsellors in local Councils on Alcoholism. The Advisory Committee on Alcoholism has suggested that, whilst such professional staff have the training and experience to respond positively, they often lack the confidence to do so. This may be partly due to uncertainty about the respective roles of the voluntary and statutory services, and partly for fear that if a problem became too difficult, specialised support would not be easily available.

These difficulties might be overcome if more time was allowed in the pre-qualification and in-service training of the professions concerned to cover the subject of alcohol misuse. But, with or without special training, most professional and voluntary staff who come into contact with people who regularly misuse alcohol would find it easier to understand the part they can play if it was generally accepted that alcohol misuse is a problem for everyone to be concerned with. The development of local group networks of workers working together in this field including those in the Prison, Probation and After-Care Service is seen by the Health Departments as an essential way of improving the ability of individual workers in the health and personal social services, and supporting voluntary agencies, to respond effectively within existing staff resources and facilities. Providing evidence of a continuing and varied pattern of support and care is the best way of encouraging people with drink problems to come forward.

The Alcohol Education Centre already organises multidisciplinary courses on alcoholism to encourage the concept of multidisciplinary working. Similar initiatives have been undertaken at the Alcohol Studies Centre at Paisley College and will shortly be undertaken at the University of Kent.

Health and local authorities can do a great deal to encourage multidisciplinary responses by developing in-service training locally in which people from different professions can be made aware of their complementary roles and responsibilities.

'Care in Action', the DHSS handbook of policies and priorities for the health and personal social services in England, has emphasised the importance of health and personal social services being responsive to local needs and changes in demand; also that decisions as to the most economical and effective use of resources are best taken by health and local authorities working together. These authorities can do a great deal to ensure that professional staff respond to demands from problem drinkers, preferably at an early stage, as part of their normal duties, using the existing range of local facilities. For its part, the Prison Service will continue in general to encourage local and regional initiatives providing support and advice where resources and facilities allow.

Help through voluntary action
Public opinion can play an important role in early intervention. People developing drinking problems need to be assured that if they take the step of

seeking help they will be heard sympathetically. While they may turn initially to voluntary organisations such as the Samaritans, awareness of more specialist agencies such as Alcoholics Anonymous (AA) or local Councils on Alcoholism can help ensure a more direct and immediate response to their approach. AA branches are located throughout the country, hold regular weekly meetings and provide a forum in which problem drinkers can share experiences and help themselves abstain from alcohol. Al-Anon and Al-Ateen are mutual support groups for relatives and teenage children of alcoholics respectively, modelled on AA.

Local Councils on Alcoholism exist in many parts of the country with trained counsellors able to help problem drinkers with constructive advice and understanding and, if necessary, to refer them to appropriate treatment agencies. These Councils depend upon voluntary support and also on help in cash and kind from the statutory services, employers and others for whom they provide a resource.

The Health Departments have been funding 'pump-priming' experiments in service provision and the results will be published to help statutory authorities decide how resources can be used effectively. The Health Departments will continue to allocate limited resources for modest experimental schemes and research projects and to promote publications of the results. There is now also the possibility of funds for innovatory service experiments coming from the Alcohol Education Research Council which is being set up under the Licensing (Alcohol Education and Research) Act 1981 (see page 36).

CHAPTER IX: Preventing alcohol misuse—the way forward

The problems

The consequences of alcohol misuse for the individual include accidents of all kinds, long term ill health, damaged family life, social isolation, loss of career and job prospects, and violence and crime. Misuse also constitutes an economic drain on the country that is indirectly detrimental to us all. The incidence of alcohol misuse and the harm it causes has increased in recent years—more rapidly among women and young people—and the numbers affected by the drinking problems of others are increasing all the time.

There are many complex reasons why individuals misuse alcohol. They may be influenced to do so by their background and upbringing, by the habits of the company they keep, by changes in social attitudes, by personal characteristics, or simply by the desire to escape some aspects of their life which upset them. The recent sharp *increase* in misuse as measured by a variety of indicators, seems clearly to be linked with the equally marked rise in overall consumption of alcohol that has occurred in the United Kingdom in recent years and the changes in people's drinking habits which underlie it.

The way forward

The first chapter of this booklet contained a summary of the scope for action in preventing alcohol misuse. This pointed to the role individuals can play by adopting sensible habits, and went on to refer to the additional measures—social, legal and fiscal—which Government can take to influence people's drinking.

The precise role the Government should play in helping prevent alcohol misuse is clearly open to debate and likely to continue to be debated for a long time to come. Many people would resist the suggestion that the degree to which people choose to put their health at risk through their drinking habits is a legitimate interest of Government. And it has to be faced that Government controls capable of effectively influencing the minority who misuse alcohol could not be established without affecting the choices available to the majority of the population who drink sensibly. Also, while the misuse of alcohol may cause serious health and social problems, the production of and trade in alcoholic drinks form an important part of our economy in terms of jobs, exports, investment, and as a source of revenue for the Government—all of which could be adversely affected by any measures designed to restrict consumption.

Nevertheless, it is important to keep in mind just what are the real costs of misuse, and how they are paid for. Certainly, those who indulge in habitual heavy drinking have to pay the cost eventually themselves; either through contracting chronic diseases such as liver cirrhosis or through becoming dependent on alcohol—that is if they are not killed or seriously injured in accidents beforehand as a result of alcohol misuse. But it is not on these people alone that the cost of their behaviour falls. There are also those whose safety is put at risk by the impaired driver or by the problem drinker at work. The social cost (not to mention personal distress and suffering) caused by family breakdown and domestic violence may be spread over many.

Alcohol may be misused by a minority but the consequences are far reaching and have to be borne by society as a whole. The services and facilities required to deal with those consequences—whether health or social services or sickness and unemployment benefit payments—not only divert resources from other—and less preventable—social problems but form part of the tax burden which has to be imposed on the nation.

The Government alone cannot secure responsible attitudes towards health matters throughout the community. To control growth in alcohol misuse and in the harm it causes requires preventive action in which central government, local government, the health professions and institutions, the business sector and trade unions, voluntary bodies, and the people of the United Kingdom as individuals can all recognise and play their separate parts. A strategy to achieve such action depends on better understanding of the issues and a general will to face up to them.

Many of the components of a preventive strategy can be established only as public debate proceeds and consensus is achieved on longer term objectives and means of achieving them. Already, however, the following items can be seen as important to any emerging strategy:

i. Programmes to help widen understanding among the general public of (i) the health risks of alcohol misuse; (ii) the social pressures which can lead to the adoption of harmful drinking habits; (iii) sensible levels of alcohol consumption; and (iv) the advantages for the young of healthy lifestyles during their school years and beyond.

ii. Specific programmes (i) to maintain publicity on the dangers of drinking and driving and the need to observe the law; and (ii) to deal with repeat offenders with excessive alcohol levels.

iii. Initiatives within firms (i) to widen understanding among the work force of the effect that impairment through drink can have on work performance and in accidents at work; (ii) to encourage problem drinkers at work to seek help; and (iii) to establish clear policies agreed between management and unions for dealing with alcohol and drinking problems at work.

iv. Action by the drinks and advertising industries (i) to improve understanding of the relative strength of drinks; and (ii) to discourage harmful drinking habits.

v. Consideration by the broadcasting authorities, programme makers, producers and writers, of ways to ensure that the presentation of alcohol on radio and TV and in films and stage plays does not unwittingly encourage bad habits.

vi. Training programmes to improve understanding among health service professionals and others in the caring professions of the extent to which drinking problems may underlie ill health and social conflicts.

vii. Continued recognition by Parliament and Government that health and social implications should be among the factors taken into account when any action affecting consumption of alcoholic drinks is under consideration.

viii. Further research studies and surveys to improve understanding of (i) social influences on attitudes to drinking; (ii) the means of affecting social influences in order to change harmful habits; (iii) factors influencing young people to drink; and (iv) circumstances associated with the development of harmful drinking habits and the onset of dependence.

Proposals have been put forward from a number of sources for some kind of permanent body with the task of ensuring that action of the various elements of a preventive strategy is effectively co-ordinated.

One suggestion (recently put forward by the National Council of Women and the Magistrates' Association) has been for a standing commission. This would have the dual task of co-ordinating policies on alcohol within Government and of presenting to Government the views of independent organisations and groups of interests concerned with prevention of alcohol misuse.

There are at present many groups and interests involved in this field which sometimes duplicate effort and at times even appear to be in competition. These include several voluntary organisations who receive funds from different sources including direct Government grants. The Government is not convinced that it is practicable or desirable to seek to supplant these independent bodies by establishing a new permanent Government appointed body. Nor is it satisfied that the establishment of formal machinery for co-ordinating Government policies is justified.

Within the central government the responsibility for policy on alcohol misuse has been allocated to DHSS, working with the other Health Departments. But several other Departments have policy responsibility for other aspects of alcohol. For example, the Home Office has the leading interest in licensing law in England and Wales; similarly the Treasury has the leading interest in policies on the taxation of alcoholic drinks; and 'sponsorship' of the alcoholic drinks industry rests with the Ministry of Agriculture, Fisheries and Food.

Well established arrangements already exist for all the interested departments to inform each other about matters of mutual concern, to co-ordinate their advice to Ministers and to implement the Government's policies. In each case, the responsibility for the necessary co-ordination rests firmly on the department with the leading interest in the aspect of policy under consideration. The Government agreees co-ordination of policy on all aspects of alcohol is essential; it believes, however, that this can be more effectively secured through the well established processes described above than by the creation of a new non-departmental public body.

The Government wishes to see progress made in tackling alcohol misuse, but the role the Government can itself play in encouraging sensible attitudes to drinking is, as previously explained, still open to debate. Of crucial importance is the ability and willingness of people to change their attitudes to alcohol misuse, and of the health professions, interested organisations, and the drinks industry itself jointly to discuss common ground and the scope they have for common action. A proposal has been put forward for a common forum, quite independent of the Government, in which all the interests—industry, voluntary bodies, professions—could be voluntarily represented. The Government would welcome the views of the bodies concerned on the prospects of making progress along these lines.

This booklet has looked at the policy issues arising on alcohol misuse, reviewed some of the options and set out what the Government at present sees as the best approach. The Government hopes that it will be widely read and discussed; and that it will assist people to clarify their minds about proper objectives of public policy and about sensible standards of private behaviour.

APPENDIX 1 Summary of recommendations in recent reports*:

Health education

Expenditure Committee
1.   A larger proportion of the revenue raised annually in duty and taxation from alcohol sales should be devoted to educating children and young adults in the dangers of alcoholic dependence.
2.   The money remaining in the Licensing Compensation Fund should be released for health education purposes.
3.   Television should be more extensively used to put across the dangers of alcohol abuse to particular identifiable groups.

Advisory Committee on Alcoholism
1.   Health education designed to alert people to the dangers of alcohol and to discourage excessive drinking should be encouraged and expanded.
2.   The presentation of alcohol to society, particularly in advertisements and the media, should be modified to produce a less one-sided picture of its effects.

Royal College of Psychiatrists
There should be a greatly enhanced Government commitment towards public education and persuasion (and relevant research), so as to bring about a reduction in drinking problems.

WHO Expert Committee
Governments should develop effective programmes of education and

* Preventine Medicine First Report from the Expenditure Committee, Session 1976-77, HMSO, London, 1977.
Report on Prevention, Advisory Committee on Alcoholism, DHSS and the Welsh Office, 1977.
Alcohol and Alcoholism, the Report of a Special Committee of the Royal College of Psychiatrists, Tavistock Publications, 1979.
Problems related to alcohol consumption, Report of a WHO Expert Committee, Technical Report Series 650, WHO, Geneva, 1980.

information about alcohol: such programmes should be specifically designed for particular segments of the general population and concerned with professional groups.

Licensing law

Expenditure Committee
The age at which alcohol is made legally available should in no circumstances be lowered.

Advisory Committee on Alcoholism
Legal restrictions on the availability of alcohol should be enforced vigorously and should not be relaxed until there is sufficient evidence that to do so would not cause increased harm.

Royal College of Psychiatrists
There should be no further relaxation of the broad range of licensing provisions.

Fiscal policy

Expenditure Committee
The price of alcoholic drink should remain at the same level relative to average income as it now is, and should not be allowed to become a relatively cheap item in the shopping basket.

Advisory Committee on Alcoholism
Fiscal powers should be utilised to ensure that alcohol does not become cheaper in real terms.

Royal College of Psychiatrists
Public revenue policies of the Government should be intentionally employed in the interest of health, so as to ensure that per capita alcohol consumption does not increase beyond the present level, and is by stages brought back to an agreed lower level.

Research

Expenditure Committee
The government should instigate, and support, research into the identification of those groups of drinkers most at risk.

Royal College of Psychiatrists
1.   The Government should commission research into the impact of liquor advertising and should be willing to curtail such advertising if the evidence warrants this.
2.   Government should take responsibility for examining the reliability of present indices of alcohol consumption and alcohol-related disabilities, their improvement, and their collation and should commission whatever additional research is necessary for the continued monitoring of preventive policies, either directly or through university departments.

Prevention strategy

Expenditure Committee
The inevitable overlap of preventive work being done by various bodies existing to counter alcoholism should be reduced by co-ordinating those bodies under one umbrella organisation.

Royal College of Psychiatrists
1.   Urgent attention should be given to means of effecting improvement in consultation and working co-operation between different departments of Government so as to ensure an integrated, effective, and evolving response to the country's drinking problems and their interrelatedness.
2.   Definite goals for preventive action should be set (eg stage one: preventing further rise in alcohol consumption and harm; stage two: reduce consumption and harm over 10 years to the levels of a decade age).
3.   The possible impact that health directed policies on alcoholism may have on the livelihood of any section of the community should be borne in mind, those interested should be consulted, and efforts should be made to devise strategies that protect these interests.

WHO Expert Committee
1.   Prevention should be given clear priority.
2.   Governments should take immediate steps to prevent any further increases in alcohol consumption.
3.   Governments should begin to reduce their per capita consumption by taking measures to reduce demand.
4.   Governments should establish co-ordinating mechanisms to implement preventive and management policies and programme and to ensure a continuing review of the situation.

APPENDIX 2 Bibliography:

This bibliography provides a general guide to the literature on alcohol misuse. Readers interested in particular aspects of the subject will find full references to other relevant works in most of the titles listed below.

General

Royal College of Psychiatrists, Alcohol and Alcoholism, Report of a Special Committee on Alcohol and Alcoholism, Tavistock, London, 1979.

World Health Organisation, Problems Related to Alcohol Consumption, Technical Report Series No 650, WHO, Geneva, 1980.

Office of Health Economics, Alcohol: Reducing the Harm, OHE, London, 1980.

Edwards, G, Grant, M (Eds), Alcoholism: New Knowledge and New Responses, Croom Helm, London, 1977.

Madden, J S, Walker, R, Kenyon, W H (Eds), Aspects of Alcohol and Drug Dependence, Pitman Medical, Tunbridge Wells, 1980.

Plant, M, Drinking Careers, Tavistock, London, 1979.

The effects of alcohol misuse

Edwards, G, Gross, M M, Kellar, M, Moser, J, Room, R (1977), Alcohol-Related Disabilities, Offset Publication 3a, WHO, Geneva, 1977.

Hore, B, Alcohol Dependence, Butterworths, London, 1976.

Jellinek, E M, The Disease Concept of Alcoholism, Hillhouse Press, New Brunswick, N J, 1960.

Sandler, M (Ed), Psychopharmacology of Alcohol, sponsored by British Association for Psychopharmacology, Raven Press, New York, 1980.

Richter, D, Addiction and Brain Damage, Croom Helm, London, 1980.

The costs of misuse

Donnan, S and Haskey, J, Population Trends, No 7, 18, 1977.

Wilson, P, Drinking in England and Wales, OPCS, HMSO, 1980.

Dight, S, Scottish Drinking Habits, OPCS, HMSO, 1976.

Blaney, R and MacKenzie, G, a Northern Ireland Community Health Study, Report to the Department of Health and Social Services, Northern Ireland, 1978.

Davies, P; British Journal on Alcohol and Alcoholism, 14, 4, pp 208-29, 1979.

Holtermann, S and Burchell, A, The Cost of Alcohol Misuse, Government Economic Service Working Paper No 37, DHSS, London, 1981.

Preventing alcohol misuse

Advisory Committee on Alcoholism, Report on Prevention, DHSS and Welsh Office, London, 1978.

House of Commons Expenditure Committee, Report on Preventive Medicine, Vols. 1-3, HMSO, London, 1977.

Davies, J and Stacey, B, Teenagers and Alcohol: a Development Study in Glasgow, Vol 2, HMSO, London, 1972.

Jahoda, G and Cramond, J, Children and Alcohol: a Development Study in Glasgow, Vol 1, HMSO, London, 1972.

Hawker, A, Adolescence and Alcohol, Edsall, London, 1978.

O'Connor, J, The Young Drinkers, Tavistock, London, 1978.

Davies, D L, Count Down on Drinking, Family Doctor Booklet, BMA, 1980.

Education and alcohol

DHSS, Addictions and Homelessness Research Liaison Group: Strategy for Research on Alcoholism, 1980.

The law

Home Office, Report of the Departmental Committee on Liquor Licensing (Erroll), HMSO, London, 1972.

Scottish Home and Health Department, Report of Department Committee on Scottish Licensing Law (Clayson), HMSO, London, 1973.

Department of the Environment, Drinking and Driving: Report of the Departmental Committee (Blennerhassett), HMSO, London, 1976.

Tax and price disincentives

Brunn K et al, Alcohol Control Policies in Public Health Perspective, Finnish Foundation for Alcohol Studies, Helsinki, 1975.

Davies, D L (Ed), the Lederman Curve, Alcohol Education Centre, London, 1977.

Early identification and help

Health and Safety Executive, The Problem Drinker at Work, HSE Occasional Paper Series: OP1, HMSO, 1980.

DHSS, Care in Action, a Handbook of Policies and Priorities for the Health and Personal Social Services in England, HMSO, London, 1980.

Larkin, E J, The Treatment of Alcoholism, Toronto,: Addiction Research Foundation, 1974.

Wilkins, R H, The Hidden Alcoholic in General Practice, ELEK Science, London.

Advisory Committee on Alcoholism, Report on Education and Training, DHSS and Welsh Office, 1979.

Advisory Committee on Alcoholism: The Pattern and Range of Services for Problem Drinkers, DHSS, and Welsh Office, 1977.

APPENDIX 3: Research

The Health Departments have limited funds available for financing research directly into aspects of problem drinking and the prevention of alcohol misuse. The DHSS Addictions and Homelessness Research Liaison Group have identified 5 priority areas for further research—identification, prevalence, prevention, treatment and the economic implications of alcohol misuse. All sound research proposals submitted to the Department will be considered for funding. High priority within the field of prevention will be given to:

a. research into the social influences on attitudes to drinking and drinking habits, and into means of affecting those influences to change attitudes and habits;

b. drinking habits among the young and factors influencing them to drink or abstain.

The Scottish Home and Health Department and the DHSS are considering also commissioning further social surveys into drinking habits following the national surveys published in 1976 and 1980 respectively.

The Health Departments keep the Medical Research Council, the Social Sciences Research Council, the Health Education Council, the Scottish Health Education Group, and other bodies able to fund research informed of their views on research priorities in this field, with the aim of exchanging ideas and encouraging complementary approaches. The Health Departments hope to enjoy similar good relations with the new Alcohol Education and Research Council when this body is set up.

Printed in England for Her Majesty's Stationery Office by Commercial Colour Press, London E.7.
Dd.717654 C50 11/81